Bible Study Guide

ED CYZEWSKI

NAVPRESS

NAVPRESS®

NavPress is the publishing ministry of The Navigators, an international Christian organization and leader in personal spiritual development. NavPress is committed to helping people grow spiritually and enjoy lives of meaning and hope through personal and group resources that are biblically rooted, culturally relevant, and highly practical.

For a free catalog go to www.NavPress.com
or call 1.800.366.7788 in the United States or 1.800.839.4769 in Canada.

© 2008 by Ed Cyzewski

ISBN-13: 978-1-60006-278-0
ISBN-10: 1-60006-278-4

Cover design by studiogearbox
Cover images by Veer

Published in association with the literary agency of Sanford Communications, Portland, Oregon.

Some of the anecdotal illustrations in this book are true to life and are included with the permission of the persons involved. All other illustrations are composites of real situations, and any resemblance to people living or dead is coincidental.

Unless otherwise identified, all Scripture quotations in this publication are taken from the HOLY BIBLE: NEW INTERNATIONAL VERSION® (NIV®). Copyright © 1973, 1978, 1984 by International Bible Society. Used by permission of Zondervan Publishing House. All rights reserved.

Printed in the United States of America

1 2 3 4 5 6 7 8 / 11 10 09 08

To my grandparents John and Phyllis Quinn

CONTENTS

FIRST THOUGHTS

With *Coffeehouse Theology*, I provided an introduction to contextual theology. If you haven't read the book yet, you might wonder, *Just what is contextual theology?* Briefly, it's the challenge of learning about God with an awareness of context, while at the same time valuing different insights from other cultures where Christians are learning about God in their own particular situations. We form contextual theology by understanding our own context and traditions and by including perspectives outside of our own, all in the midst of our study of the Bible.

While you can find a number of great books written on a scholarly level by leading contextual theologians, the goal of *Coffeehouse Theology* is to provide a bridge to connect their work with today's church.

However, because I often reduced and simplified complex issues and rarely had opportunity to dig into a thorough study of Scripture verses in the main book, I also want to help you explore several key Scripture passages that show how you can actively participate in a contextual theology that leads to kingdom action. The goal of this Bible study guide is to help you (and others you meet within a small group or Sunday school class setting) take these first steps.

HOW TO USE THIS GUIDE

This Bible study workbook is actually one of two study guides that can help you apply what you've learned from *Coffeehouse Theology*. The other study guide, *Coffeehouse Theology: Contemporary Issues Discussion Guide*, will help you put the thoughts of global and historic theologians regarding a variety of pressing issues to best use in theology today. The study guide you're holding begins with biblical passages and then works through a series of discussion questions and commentaries. After reading a chapter of *Coffeehouse Theology* (or in the case of session 4, two chapters), you can find the corresponding session in this guide and dig deeper while also learning how to put a sound method of contextual theology into practice. In each session, you'll

- walk through some relevant contextual issues,
- meditate on a pertinent passage from the Bible,
- consider a few words of my commentary to jumpstart your thinking,
- ponder brief but valuable insights from historic or global Christians,
- discuss some ways to apply the issue to the mission of God's kingdom,
- begin exploring ways to live out your theology in your daily life.

Through *Coffeehouse Theology* and this Bible study guide, you'll quickly catch on to simple ways to form and to live out theology today. Allow me to share a few thoughts that will help you and your group get the most out of each session:

- Study the entire chapter from which the selected verses in the session are taken. In fact, I suggest that you read the chapters preceding and following the quoted chapter. Better yet, pick up *The Message* or the New Living Translation and read the entire book of Scripture to gain an idea of where the passage you're studying fits in with the author's main ideas.
- Don't try to answer every single question. We all learn in different ways. The same holds true when it comes to how we approach

theology. You and the other people in your discussion group might come at theology from a variety of angles, so I've done my best to provide a wide range of questions. But don't worry; I won't be handing out grades after you complete this study!

- Tackle the hard questions. When a question seems especially unsettling, that's one you should try to answer, even if it means taking some extra time to work through it.

- Remind yourself that your faith rests on the revelation of Jesus Christ, the Son of God. That will allow you to hold up assumptions, personally important issues, and particular doctrines to greater degrees of scrutiny. You might find that God is quite different from your personal sketches of him — I know that I've discovered some fresh and revealing insights about God through studies like this one.

- Pay special attention to the "Living Out Your Theology" section at the end of each session. This section will help you get theology out of your head and into your heart and hands and feet. This section will help you become aware of the best ways to share the gospel and of the greatest needs your ministries can meet.

WHY JUMP IN?

Again, this study guide aims to help you learn how to put contextual theology into practice. Each session will help you reflect on the main points of *Coffeehouse Theology* while also working through some of theology's contextual, biblical, historic, and global aspects. Please keep in mind that understanding and even forming theology isn't limited to "professional" theologians. In fact, a growing conversation is taking place in the local, global, and historic church, led by the Spirit of God as his people study his inspired Scripture, seek to know him, and join him in the work of his kingdom.

Ed Cyzewski

ACKNOWLEDGMENTS

I'm deeply grateful to Caleb Seeling of NavPress for taking the time to discuss the idea of this study guide with me and for helping me put together some practical ideas on how to provide a simple step from the ideas of *Coffeehouse Theology* into everyday, practical theology. My editor, Brad Lewis, did much to sharpen my ideas and bridge the study guide with the main book. I'm greatly indebted to his masterful synthesis of ideas. My wife, Julie, provided timely and indispensable support in both researching and reading through the manuscript, and I do not exaggerate when I say this guide is much better than I could have imagined thanks to her hard work and insights.

GETTING STARTED

The Supremacy of Love

To get the most out of this session,
I suggest reading the introduction in Coffeehouse Theology.

I want to start at the end.

At the end of the introduction to *Coffeehouse Theology*, I point out that theology's far-reaching influence into our everyday lives calls us into a careful consideration of just where our beliefs come from. And in the final chapter of the book, I point out that love—loving God and loving one another—stands as the ultimate goal of theology.

I'd like to ground all of theology in this very Christian practice of loving God and loving one another. Good theology should point to love as the highest goal. Theology that doesn't result in greater love becomes a futile exercise in accumulating knowledge. If theology is truly about learning to love God in deeper ways, then love should be at the forefront of our minds during our first steps in theological study. As a result, when we live out our theology in practical ways, we should see arguments, division, and bitterness decrease while love, dialogue, unity, and diversity increase. Unless we measure success by this second list, theology will never help the church embody God's kingdom here on earth.

CONTEXT: LOVE AND UNITY IN TODAY'S WORLD

The willingness to look at both culture and context as we form and then live out our theology plays a central role in *Coffeehouse Theology*. Context simply means your situation—the "where you are" that's a part of making you "who you are." While context is somewhat individual, culture might be described as "the way of life for an entire society," including "codes of manners, dress, language, religion, rituals, norms of behavior, . . . and systems of belief."[1]

And of course, we also look to the Bible as a primary source as we form our theology.

In chapters 4 and 5 of *Coffeehouse Theology*, I address the culture's shift from a modern context to a postmodern one. Surprisingly, these philosophical concepts can teach us a lot about Christian unity and love. Speaking in broad terms, certainty was the goal in the modern context, while today's postmodern culture has room for ambiguity and dialogue. The danger in the modern context was disagreement and division, while the pitfall in the postmodern world is a noncommittal relativism that refuses to take a position on important topics.

I bring up these weighty philosophical movements because, whether we like it or not, they radically shape how we think and interact with one another. If the goal is absolute certainty when it comes to theology, then we'll find it much more difficult to love and accept people who hold perspectives that differ from ours. However, if the goal is dialogue and working toward the truth with room for a variety of views, we have a framework that creates space for love in the midst of disagreements.

With this context in mind, ponder and discuss the following questions:

- When dealing with theology, are you more comfortable with certainty or uncertainty? When might uncertainty be appropriate for theologians?

- Why do you think Christians argue about theology?

- As budding theologians, how should we balance love and unity with theological disagreements?

MEDITATION

Take some time to meditate on 1 Corinthians 13:8-13 and then discuss the questions that follow:

> Love never fails. But where there are prophecies, they will cease; where there are tongues, they will be stilled; where there is knowledge, it will pass away. For we know in part and we prophesy in part, but when perfection comes, the imperfect disappears. When I was a child, I talked like a child, I thought like a child, I reasoned like a child. When I became a man, I put childish ways behind me. Now we see but a poor reflection as in a mirror; then we shall see face to face. Now I know in part; then I shall know fully, even as I am fully known.
>
> And now these three remain: faith, hope and love. But the greatest of these is love.

- How would you define the words *faith*, *hope*, and *love* in this passage? Which do most churches today seem to show? Why?

- Why do you think the apostle Paul said "the greatest of these is love"?

- Think about what's most important to you and to your Christian community. How would placing love above everything else change your community?

MY THOUGHTS

Today's church romanticizes the early church as happily meeting in homes in a state of unity under the godly teachings of Paul, the super-apostle. In fact, in some Christian quarters today, churches have a fascination with going back to the ways of the early church. However, the truth is that the early church was full of quarrels, debates, divisions, and groups that refused to get along. In addition to theological disputes, early Christians also struggled with a racial tension among Jews and Gentiles who were suddenly expected to worship the same God after hundreds of bitter years of avoiding each other. In fact, the early church could have split in innumerable ways.

Now that we've got the background straight, let's talk about meat. I grew up in a home where meat was the main ingredient of just about every meal. Americans (by which I mean citizens of the United States of America) love cheap meat, and producers have developed an entire system to provide the cheapest meat possible to consumers. No matter how this system affects the streams and fields — not to mention the hormones and slop stuck into the animals crammed into buildings where they stand in their own filth — the modern meat industry delivers the cheap meat that Americans crave for their meals. Even if locally purchased, grass-fed animals provide healthier meat and probably keep the environment in better shape, price becomes the ultimate determiner for many people who can't afford pricey organic products.

If Americans are willing to purchase meat injected with antibiotics and raised in questionable conditions, then we should be able to relate to the problems Paul had with meat during the days of the early church. Instead of dealing with chemicals or conditions on a feedlot, Paul struggled to find a godly path through the issue of meat sacrificed to idols. With so much meat left over from the sacrifices to false gods who didn't have much use for animal flesh, the Greeks established a system of selling the sacrificed meat at a reduced rate. This was almost like joining together the temple of the local gods and a Sam's Club. Savvy Christian shoppers could eat well while saving quite a bit of money.

However, this method of shopping didn't sit well with some recent converts to Christianity from pagan religions, who struggled to separate the meat from the worship of idols. Imagine the confusion that arose when Christians gathered for the Lord's Supper (or Communion, which was a meal back then) and placed in front of them was meat that had been sacrificed to idols! In the midst of a Christian act of worship, they faced the idolatry they'd left. Meanwhile, other Christians had no trouble eating this meat because they were confident these fictitious gods posed no threat to their faith in God.

Enter Paul.

Think of the kid you knew who always found his way into trouble, spent a lot of time in the principal's office, and yet possessed irresistible charm and moments of brilliance, and you'll have a rough sketch of the Corinthian church and its relationship with Paul, the parent with graying hair. God had granted the Corinthian Christians incredible gifts of healing, prophecy, and teaching. But they abused these gifts, struggled to maintain unity, and even looked down on Paul, whom they considered unimpressive and timid. The apostle, however, exerted much time and energy to bring this wayward church back in line with the love of Christ and the gospel. When those troubled by the meat sacrificed to idols spoke up, they were largely ignored by those who claimed to possess superior knowledge.

In 1 Corinthians 10:24, Paul attacks this rampant individualism and theological snobbery with this simple principle: "Nobody should seek his own good, but the good of others." While avoiding a black-and-white condemnation of one group or the other, Paul points this church to love, proclaiming that love should guide every aspect of their lives and worship. Because God called Christians to glorify him in all they do, Paul reminds the Corinthian brothers and sisters to avoid offending each other by following the example of Christ (see 1 Corinthians 10:31-33).

I find it amazing that through the centuries since Paul wrote these words about Christian unity, some Christians have used 1 Corinthians 13 to foster other divisions in the church. Some factions use this chapter to argue against the continuation of prophecy, healing, and tongues after the apostolic period. Others take Paul's statement about knowledge fading away and all of our pithy little beliefs amounting to little more than the reflection of a dim mirror as proof that serious Christian scholarship is of little value. So I have to ask, are we really catching on to this passage and Paul's focus on Christian unity?

Sometimes I can't help wondering if we're hopeless. Far from laying out what was in or out for the church, Paul cut through all of the petty squabbles and established love as the supreme way for the church to thrive. If we really dig into the story behind this epistle, we see a church not so different from our own today, and we'll find Paul's words oddly . . . relevant, as he commands the church to follow the way of love (see 1 Corinthians 14:1).

Fortunately Paul doesn't stop with correcting the Corinthian Christians for failing to remain unified. He shows them the most excellent path to follow no matter what the situation: love. It might have been much easier if the apostle simply provided a list of what's approved and what's taboo. But instead Paul points this troubled church to love—and God desires that Christians today follow that same path toward unity.

INSIGHTS FROM THE HISTORIC/GLOBAL CHURCH

The great church father Augustine made a radical statement that chafes against the desire of some Christians to be right instead of being united or loving: "When interpreted correctly, all Scripture leads to love of God and one's neighbor."[2] I find that many American Christians make it their business to protect Christianity, to guard the Bible, and to fight a battle against secular culture in order to preserve a Christianized version of our society. This combative outlook runs counter to the biblical witness, pitting God's chosen people against the people we're supposed to serve as ambassadors of God's kingdom. While we should always speak the truth as Christians, an unnecessary level of antagonism arises when we speak of defending the Bible or the truth. Instead of focusing solely on arriving at the correct doctrine, Augustine set his sights on reflecting the character of the God he studied.

In his book *The Heavenly Man* (London: Monarch, 2002), Chinese house church leader Brother Yun shares how the Chinese church struggled through a difficult period of division. When Western Christians began smuggling Bibles into China, they added the bonus of books about doctrine. Over the course of time, the Chinese church split along the lines specified in these theology books to the point that certain church leaders would hardly stay in the same room together. Brother Yun worked tirelessly to bridge the splits destroying the Chinese church and eventually succeeded. He not only managed to bring various leaders together, but one prominent pastor humbly washed the feet of a rival. This landmark moment marked the beginning of a sorely needed period of reconciliation in the church. In the end, the love of God conquered the supposedly superior knowledge of differing denominations, as they united in their love for and fellowship with Christ.

APPLYING TO MISSION

- If good theology "leads to love of God and one's neighbor," as Augustine stated, what needs to change when we form theology?

- Do you have any contact with someone who holds a low opinion of Christians? If appropriate, ask this person to express his or her opinion about Jesus and Christians. Don't argue — your objective is to listen and learn.

- What group in your area needs to experience the love of God? This might be a socioeconomic group or some other demographic category of individuals. List one or two of these groups and then brainstorm ways you can demonstrate the love of God to them. (Hint: Think beyond a simple gospel presentation.)

LIVING OUT YOUR THEOLOGY

- Have you been burned by a Christian who failed to love, or have you failed to love a fellow Christian? What was the central issue of your argument or division?

- How can you increase your dialogue with Christians from other backgrounds?

- What five theological issues are most important to you? How can you hold on to these doctrines while also preserving unity and love with Christians who disagree with you?

THEOLOGY FROM THE INSIDE OUT

To get the most out of this session,
I suggest reading chapter 1 in Coffeehouse Theology.

At rock bottom, Christianity is a story about God reconciling himself with the disobedient children of the human race. The love and mercy of God take center stage as he invites humanity to enter his kingdom, where his healing and justice reign. Jesus proclaimed that God's kingdom is very much present in this world; when Jesus returned to heaven, he left his followers the task of living under and declaring God's present and imminent rule and inviting one and all to enter. For Christians carrying out this mission today, theology becomes their vital tool. The kingdom of God isn't just the content of Christian theology. It's the driving force.

CONTEXT: AMERICANS AND THE KINGDOM OF GOD

As Americans who live in a democratic society, we can easily misunderstand the nature of God's kingdom and his rule. We're used to having a say in our government, so handing over control to an all-powerful ruler seems terrifying, no matter how benevolent he may seem.

While we struggle to re-create the mood of the prophecies concerning the coming of God's rule, for the most part the focus of God's kingdom is a reunion with his beloved people and the establishment of true justice and peace. Far from establishing a cruel dictatorship, God delights in his people and wants to bring healing to the nations. Of course, this can only happen if we drop our own agendas—which typically put us first—and submit to his rule.

While most people readily agree that all is not as it should be in this world, the tough part is getting the same people to admit that God's plan is the one to follow. Americans especially seem convinced of their own goodness and excellent intentions. To make matters worse, many American Christians ally themselves tightly with political parties, committing resources to flawed, man-made methods of bringing God's kingdom to earth.

What's more, if this overall allegiance to man-made institutions isn't bad enough, many American Christians create their own little kingdoms within their denominations or local churches. Theology often gets caught up in the tangled mess of these hefty organizations that eat up time and resources. Instead of helping Christians spread the gospel and live in the reality of God's kingdom among people who need both so badly, theology serves the agenda of these smaller kingdoms, providing the ammunition for internal disputes and unending debates. Most of us find it much too tempting to cling to our own plans. But as a result, we restrict theology to our internal concerns instead of using theology to draw near to God, to live in the reality of his rule, and to spread the message of the kingdom.

With this context in mind, ponder and discuss the following questions:

- Use a Bible concordance and look up three passages in the gospels where Jesus talks about the kingdom of God or the kingdom of heaven. How is the kingdom different from the church?

- List three theological doctrines that you believe have a powerful influence on your faith. How do they affect the way you share the gospel?

- Tell your "salvation story" in a few paragraphs. How has theology changed your understanding of God since you first began your relationship with Christ?

MEDITATION

Take some time to meditate on Isaiah 42:1-7 and Luke 4:18-19 and then discuss the questions that follow:

"Here is my servant, whom I uphold,
    my chosen one in whom I delight;
I will put my Spirit on him
    and he will bring justice to the nations.
He will not shout or cry out
    or raise his voice in the streets.
A bruised reed he will not break,
    and a smoldering wick he will not snuff out.
In faithfulness he will bring forth justice;
    he will not falter or be discouraged
till he establishes justice on earth.
    In his law the islands will put their hope."

This is what God the LORD says—
he who created the heavens and stretched them out,
    who spread out the earth, and all that comes out of it,
who gives breath to its people,
    and life to those who walk on it:
"I, the LORD, have called you in righteousness;
    I will take hold of your hand.
I will keep you and will make you
    to be a covenant for the people
    and a light for the Gentiles,
to open eyes that are blind,
    to free captives from prison
    and to release from the dungeon those who sit in darkness."
    (Isaiah 42:1-7)

"The Spirit of the Lord is on me,
    because he has anointed me
    to preach good news to the poor.
He has sent me to proclaim freedom for the prisoners
    and recovery of sight for the blind,
to release the oppressed,
    to proclaim the year of the Lord's favor." (Luke 4:18-19)

• Did Jesus bring justice as these passages suggest? How?

- How do you think the original readers interpreted these passages compared to how we read them today? Do you think Christians today overly spiritualize these verses? How?

- What role do the people of God play in these passages?

MY THOUGHTS

Easter is one of my favorite Christian feasts because I love the story of Jesus' resurrection. Celebrating the Resurrection is as good as it gets for Christians, because the event heralds the new life and freedom won by Christ. The only damper on this celebration of new life and salvation, in my opinion, is the church.

In many churches, Easter Sunday ends up being an awkward time. The irregular attendees known as "Easter People" show up in their best Sunday clothes, while the regulars sit smugly and wait for the preacher to roast these people who like God a lot but only as friends. Easter morning often becomes the primary ambush time to drop the full weight of the gospel message on the Easter People who clog up the parking lot and drink all the coffee. I remember spending many Easters glaring at the new faces in the crowd and thinking, *You're really in for it now.* The Easter People quickly realize they must pass through the sermon gamut: God loves you and has a wonderful plan for you that includes attending *this* church and saying *this* prayer to be saved.

The worst Easter morning I ever experienced involved a long, elaborate, and technical explanation of just how salvation works. The preacher hauled out words such as *atonement* and *propitiation*, spending enormous amounts of time defining them, setting them up, and then reconnecting them with his main point, which ambled toward saying a prayer at the end of the service. As a theology student, I could follow his lengthy treatise. But even I was bored and uninspired, so I wondered how our church's guests felt that day.

Sadly, we've somehow managed to lose the incredible story of God's rescuing humanity from death by conquering it from the inside, substituting abstract doctrines and a mechanical, step-by-step salvation process. We focus so closely on a few crucial details that we lose the grand narrative and immense scope of salvation.

In Luke 4:14-30, Jesus isn't preaching on an Easter morning. But he does make a strong connection to the prophecy in Isaiah 42 about his mission to bring righteousness and justice to Israel and ultimately to the entire world. Christians who spend their Easter mornings listening to sermons about receiving the death of Jesus in order to go to heaven—and I include myself with this group—aren't quite sure what to do with Jesus' message about proclaiming freedom for prisoners, recovering the sight for the blind, or releasing the oppressed.

The gospel of John reminds us that Jesus' ministry combined *physical signs* that pointed to deeper *spiritual truths*. The spiritually blind and oppressed people of Israel needed spiritual vision, but Jesus also healed people who were blind physically. Both the physical and spiritual pointed to the arrival of God's kingdom and a new way of interpreting their role as God's chosen people through the ministry, death, and resurrection of Jesus.[1] While those who follow Jesus indeed enjoy eternal benefits, the passage from Isaiah suggests something significant is also taking place in our world right now. The rule of God has dawned.

Far from simply establishing a message about spiritual change through accepting a new doctrine or praying a prayer, Jesus' mission reached more broadly and deeply into the lives of his listeners. He also called for a new world with greater freedom and justice resulting from the spiritual change brought about when people learn to love God and one another. Jesus not only redefined the terms of knowing God—as a Father or parent—he brought the beginning of God's rule on earth.

INSIGHTS FROM THE HISTORIC/GLOBAL CHURCH

In the Philippines, farmers have suffered the loss of their lands and watched a few wealthy individuals accumulate wealth at the expense of the many poor. After selling off their lands to large farming conglomerations, many of these farmers go hungry while feeding the rest of the world. In this context, the message of Luke 4:19 jumps off the page to offer hope in ways few Americans would ever consider.

Theologian Helen R. Graham points to the implications of Jesus' message in Luke 4:19 concerning the year of the Lord's favor or the year of Jubilee. Jesus refers to Leviticus 25:8-54, where God commands Israel not only to take a year off from planting, but also to return all land to the original owners.[2] Because of this command, no one could accumulate vast amounts of land and the wealth that would result. God proclaimed, "The land must not be sold permanently, because the land is mine and you are but aliens and my tenants. Throughout the country that you hold as a possession, you must provide for the redemption of the land" (Leviticus 25:23-24). I wonder how that would preach on a Sunday morning in America.

APPLYING TO MISSION

- What social problems does your church or ministry work to remedy? Why does your church focus on these issues?

- Reread Luke 4:18-19. How do you think your church interprets and applies these verses? Can you think of any ways that your church needs to change its approach to the poor and other social issues?

- If your church is located in a relatively affluent area, contact a church or ministry leader in an area without the same kind of wealth. Ask this leader how he or she interprets Luke 4:18-19 and how your church can better apply this passage.

LIVING OUT YOUR THEOLOGY

- Can you think of a richer way to share the gospel message (as opposed to the four-minute, shrink-wrapped version) in light of Jesus' proclamation in Luke 4?

- Review the list of your three most important theological issues (from the "Context" section of this session). What theological issues are you unclear about — either you haven't considered them or you haven't landed on what you believe? Reflect on your list and discuss these issues with your group as you continue through this study guide.

- Talk with others in your group about how to balance the doctrine of life after death with the doctrine of the kingdom of God being established on earth now.

HOW TO DO CHRISTIAN THEOLOGY

To get the most out of this session,
I suggest reading chapter 2 in Coffeehouse Theology.

Christian theology is informed by the movement of God's salvation plan from the beginning of God's people in Genesis, through the Exodus, Exile, and coming of Jesus the Messiah. Though the cast of characters changes from book to book, the one constant is God, the one who works to restore fallen creation to a relationship with him. From Abraham to Mary, God takes the initiative by revealing himself and carrying people through seemingly impossible, hopeless situations. The Christian New Testament was finalized in the fourth century after Christ and provides accurate accounts of this salvation story. Outside of these books are the creeds, councils, and other church documents that reveal how the church at particular points in history understood God and the story of reconciliation. Today the global church still wrestles with forming theology, each Christian community throughout the world providing a particular perspective from specific traditions.

Though there is no official way to create theology, an informed approach to Christian theology today should take into account each of these important parts: God, Scripture, tradition, and the global church. Interpreting the Bible is dangerous business, as mistakes can cause deep rifts in society and unimaginable social wrongs. Need I mention the Crusades, the Inquisition, or the Salem Witch Trials, among a long list of Christian atrocities throughout history?

CONTEXT: SEEKING THE VOICE OF GOD

At the age of twelve, I began to read the Bible. I attended a Baptist church on Sunday mornings and also attended a Catholic parish on Saturday evenings. During this time, I met with a Catholic priest who expressed his concern that Baptists read the Bible outside the authority of the church. He said that they could make the Bible say whatever they want, and even described this as "dangerous."

From my limited perspective, the friendly people in my Baptist church took the worship of God very seriously, studied the Bible, and did their best to obey the teachings of God. In fact, when I looked at my Catholic friends who generally didn't care about the Bible and the relative boredom of a one-hour (forty-five minutes if you were lucky) Catholic mass, I couldn't help concluding that Baptists were the authentic followers of Jesus. Still, the words of that priest stuck in my mind: "Interpreting the Bible on your own is dangerous."

Fifteen years after that conversation, I have to admit that I agree with his diagnosis, that studying the Bible on your own — even within a church — is dangerous. However, I differ when it comes to the solution. I think we run into danger when small groups of Christians study the Bible on their own and then say their findings are the authoritative truth of God. When I hear Christians say, "Here's what God says about . . . ," I start to worry. Confusing our own interpretations with the very teachings of God can lead to all manner of abuse, guilt, condemnation, and flat-out false teachings.

My remedy for the dangers of interpreting Scripture is combining four sources of theology: God, Scripture, tradition, and the global church. The revelation of God's Spirit and Scripture itself provide the primary sources of theology. Our traditions and the global church ground us in the universal voice of God, reminding us we can't figure out God on our own. Our traditions often help us have sort of a baseline, but we need to add the perspective of global Christians to teach us that God and Scripture possess many layers of meaning. The end result of combining these sources: a humbler and gentler theology that still pursues truth, even if the truth is more complex than we could ever imagine.

With this context in mind, ponder and discuss the following questions:

- Out of the four sources I suggest for forming theology — God, Scripture, tradition, and the global church — which do you give highest priority? Why?

- In the book I use the metaphor of a collaborative street mural to describe the ongoing and communal act of theology. Discuss what this means. Can you think of other metaphors for forming theology that resonate with you?

- What are some of the roles and purposes of theology?

MEDITATION

Take some time to meditate on Acts 15:5-18 and then discuss the questions that follow:

Then some of the believers who belonged to the party of the Pharisees stood up and said, "The Gentiles must be circumcised and required to obey the law of Moses."

The apostles and elders met to consider this question. After much discussion, Peter got up and addressed them: "Brothers, you know that some time ago God made a choice among you that the Gentiles might hear from my lips the message of the gospel and believe. God, who knows the heart, showed that he accepted them by giving the Holy Spirit to them, just as he did to us. He made no distinction between us and them, for he purified their hearts by faith. Now then, why do you try to test God by putting on the necks of the disciples a yoke that neither we nor our fathers have been able to bear? No! We believe it is through the grace of our Lord Jesus that we are saved, just as they are."

The whole assembly became silent as they listened to Barnabas and Paul telling about the miraculous signs and wonders God had done among the Gentiles through them. When they finished, James spoke up: "Brothers, listen to me. Simon has described to us how God at first showed his concern by taking from the Gentiles a people for himself. The words of the prophets are in agreement with this, as it is written:

"'After this I will return
    and rebuild David's fallen tent.
Its ruins I will rebuild,
    and I will restore it,
that the remnant of men may seek the Lord,
    and all the Gentiles who bear my name,
says the Lord, who does these things
    that have been known for ages.'"

- This might be the first theological dispute in the early church. What evidence did Barnabas and Paul provide to help settle the dispute? How do miracles figure in to the decision made by the church?

- Read Amos 9:11-12 and Isaiah 45:20-21 (take special note of Amos 9:12). How do these verses apply to the situation confronting the early church? What does this reveal about the early church's use of Scripture? What do you think it says about the way we interpret Scripture today?

MY THOUGHTS

I love what happens in this passage of Scripture when the church needs to take a stand on the issue of "Judaizing" the Gentiles. First, the church leaders find out where God stands on the matter. Interestingly, they don't turn to the Bible as their first source. Peter begins by pointing to God's approval of the Gentiles "just as they are" based on a vision and the outpouring of the Holy Spirit on Gentile believers. Then Paul adds a global perspective by verifying God's revelation through miracles and the manifestation of the Holy Spirit among Gentile believers. Once the church leaders reached a consensus on God's will, they then checked Scripture to ensure that their current revelation matched what Scripture declared. And as God's will, the Spirit's working among believers, and Scripture all lined up, the church's decision to allow Gentiles to worship God without adhering to Jewish restrictions became a foregone conclusion.

Of course, our theological debates today rarely come to such a smooth resolution. Typically, missionaries and global Christians aren't on hand to offer different perspectives. Our traditions vary widely. And many theologians don't believe that we can observe physical manifestations of God's Spirit — not to mention miracles, tongues, and tiny flames on people's heads.

In addition, we also need to question how closely we should follow this account as a model for our theology today. We need to remember that Luke wrote as a historian describing a situation in the early church and not necessarily as a theologian providing strict guidelines for us to follow. So just how should we put this important passage into practice today?

I suggest that we view the Bible as a portrait illustrating the way people knew God at a particular time and place, and not necessarily as a strict blueprint to follow. When we make the Bible into a blueprint or strict guidebook to follow, we tend to pick and choose commands that match up with our own preferences, and we conveniently forget about the parts that don't fit with our own beliefs. That's why I hesitate to say that this passage tells us exactly how to deal with every doctrinal dispute, because doing so would be unrealistic and ultimately abuses the Bible. But I can say that this passage teaches us how resolving theological disputes can take place, and it definitely provides some clues about important issues to consider when forming theology. In other words, if we refuse to consider God's revelation, if we avoid looking at Scripture, or if we ignore the input of global Christians, we should at least pause and consider our ways. When I look at Acts 15, I see the church gathering together under the influence of God's Spirit, listening to a variety of voices, and checking them against the solid revelation of Scripture. This portrait of Christians forming theology informs and guides how we can make similar decisions today.

As we look back through history, we can see that Christians sometimes made grievous errors in the name of Christ. Often these mistakes occurred because the church refused to listen to diverse voices, ignored the Spirit of God, or failed to consider key Scripture passages. So as we practice contextual theology, I urge us to pay attention to the church of Acts 15. As we take into account context, Christian tradition, the global church, and base theology on God himself as revealed in Scripture, we can ensure that we're following a well-balanced approach to theology—one informed by the practice of Peter, Paul, and James, even if it's not a perfect copy.

INSIGHTS FROM THE HISTORIC/GLOBAL CHURCH

At the end of the second century, the Christian theologian Irenaeus confronted numerous heresies of his time through his work, "Against Heresies." When one particular group claimed special revelations concerning Scripture that ran counter to the traditions of the church, Irenaus replied:

Yet when we appeal once more to that tradition which is from the apostles, safeguarded in the churches by successions of presbyters, we provoke these into becoming the enemies of traditions, claiming to be wiser than those presbyters, and even the apostles themselves, and to have discovered the undefiled truth. . . . Thus they end up agreeing with neither the Scriptures not with tradition. . . . Everyone who wishes to perceive the truth should consider the apostolic tradition, which has been made known in every church in the entire world.[1]

When comparing Irenaeus to Acts 15, we see quite a different method of determining correct doctrine, as he directly refers to the teachings passed down from the apostles as the key authority. Of course, the heretics in question claimed a kind of special revelation from God, so the role of tradition would be seen to carry greater weight. Wherever we end up in our views on Scripture, tradition, and the other sources of theology, Irenaeus reminds us that theologians have been wrestling with and hammering out correct doctrines for all of church history.

APPLYING TO MISSION

- What theological challenges have you faced when sharing the gospel or discipling new Christians? Compare your approach to these challenges with the situation the early church faced in Acts 15.

- How do you think ministry and theology are connected? Explain.

LIVING OUT YOUR THEOLOGY

- In Acts 15, how did the Holy Spirit and miracles factor into the church's decision? How does this compare to the way you make decisions about your theological beliefs?

- Do you think manifestations of the Holy Spirit and miracles fit into theology today? How?

Session 3

CHRISTIANITY IS EMBEDDED IN CULTURE . . . NOW WHAT?

*To get the most out of this session,
I suggest reading chapter 3 in* Coffeehouse Theology.

For better or worse, Christianity is embedded into culture. Because there's no "culture-free" expression of the gospel,[1] Christians must wrestle with the complexities of embodying the message of Christ in a particular time and place.

We will benefit greatly through an ongoing dialogue between faith and culture that doesn't pit them against each other. Our faith needs the insights of our times, while the world needs the words of life delivered by the gospel. Of course, our goal is to deliver those words of life — always representing God's kingdom and spreading his message of hope that salvation and renewal has entered this world. We are the heralds of God's redemption and revolution of hope.[2] We simply use the insights of our times — our culture's terminology and categories — while still challenging the broken systems of the world.

CONTEXT: AMERICAN CHRISTIANITY AND CULTURE

Culture has become something to fight against in America. Christians speak of fighting culture wars, which basically means intellectual and political battles over topics such as evolution, abortion, gay rights, prayer in schools, and atheism. In fact, Americans like nothing better than a good fight, and maybe we even overuse the word *war*: Think War on Drugs, War on Poverty, and War on Terror. Give us something worth opposing, and we'll fight a war against it. And so Christians encounter atheists, abortion rights activists, and other groups challenging the role of Christianity in society today and promptly declare war.

I used to be a culture warrior. I saw culture as a force opposed to Christianity, and any values of "the world" (essentially another name for non-Christian culture) had no place in my theology. I supported politicians who advanced a supposedly Christian agenda warring against the secular forces trying to steer our nation down a path of immorality and godlessness, because I worried that the result would be judgment and doom for America. I learned about the faith of our Founding Fathers, dug up quotes about the importance of God to America's politics, and opposed anyone who hinted that America isn't a Christian nation.

At the time, I didn't realize how captive I really was to culture—how I'd mixed my Christianity with a particular conservative culture and had ended up fighting a phony war. The truth is that when we try to link God's kingdom to any political party or nation, we lose the "war" long before the fighting even begins. Jesus isn't a conservative, a liberal, or an American. Rather, he cuts through all cultural divides to spread the message of God's kingdom from the bottom up—eschewing the halls of power, yet challenging the powers and injustices of our world.

The message of God's kingdom addresses the issues of our times from God's perspective but refuses to be limited to one side in some supposed culture war. We begin to wade through this mess toward a solution when we first acknowledge that we do have preferences, that we have taken sides, and that we need to work on overcoming these limitations. We live in a culture that we must learn about, sometimes put to use, and at other times oppose.

We can't simply isolate ourselves from our culture or fight it as a cohesive enemy. At the same time, we can't associate the kingdom of God with any political agenda. Instead, the key to connecting Christianity and culture lies in learning to dialogue between God's authority and revelation through Scripture and the peculiar influences of our times. We're seeking a relevant contextual theology that also bears the prophetic message of God in our times. Forming a theologically faithful but culturally aware theology is the challenge of the church today.

With this context in mind, ponder and discuss the following questions:

- What difficulties have you experienced in overcoming cultural differences with others?

- Describe three values you believe are important that come from your culture. How might these affect your theology?

- What are some practical ways you can increase your awareness of your culture?

MEDITATION

Take some time to meditate on Matthew 22:15-22 and Luke 20:19-26 and then discuss the questions that follow:

Then the Pharisees went out and laid plans to trap him in his words. They sent their disciples to him along with the Herodians. "Teacher," they said, "we know you are a man of integrity and that you teach the way of God in accordance with the truth. You aren't swayed by men, because you pay no attention to who they are. Tell us then, what is your opinion? Is it right to pay taxes to Caesar or not?"

But Jesus, knowing their evil intent, said, "You hypocrites, why are you trying to trap me? Show me the coin used for paying the tax." They brought him a denarius, and he asked them, "Whose portrait is this? And whose inscription?"

"Caesar's," they replied.

Then he said to them, "Give to Caesar what is Caesar's, and to God what is God's."

When they heard this, they were amazed. So they left him and went away. (Matthew 22:15-22)

The teachers of the law and the chief priests looked for a way to arrest him immediately, because they knew he had spoken this parable against them. But they were afraid of the people.

Keeping a close watch on him, they sent spies, who pretended to be honest. They hoped to catch Jesus in something he said so that they might hand him over to the power and authority of the governor. So the spies questioned him: "Teacher, we know that you speak and teach what is right, and that you do not show partiality but teach the way of God in accordance with the truth. Is it right for us to pay taxes to Caesar or not?"

He saw through their duplicity and said to them, "Show me a denarius. Whose portrait and inscription are on it?"

"Caesar's," they replied.

He said to them, "Then give to Caesar what is Caesar's, and to God what is God's."

They were unable to trap him in what he had said there in public. And astonished by his answer, they became silent. (Luke 20:19-26)

- What differences do you see between Matthew's and Luke's accounts?

- If you'd been in Jesus' shoes, how would you have responded to the question the Pharisees asked?

- What was at stake with Jesus' answer?

MY THOUGHTS

Jesus knew his times well. For that matter, so did Matthew and Luke. Most scholars believe that Matthew wrote his gospel for a Jewish audience, while Luke—who addressed his gospel to Theophilus the Greek—directed his gospel at a wider, Gentile audience. Matthew often wrote about different holidays and factions of the Jews with no explanation, while Luke often explained the Jewish culture or omitted Jewish details if the narrative didn't require them. Further, Matthew carried the burden of proving that Jesus was the Messiah who fulfilled Old Testament prophecies despite being opposed to many of the religious leaders of his day. On the other hand, Luke advanced the case for Jesus' being the Son of God and Savior of the world by sharing many of Matthew's same stories, but with subtle shifts of focus.

In this particular passage, Matthew carefully notes the plotting of two Jewish groups, Herodians (who conspired with the Roman occupation force) and Pharisees (religious leaders who opposed the Romans), to capture Jesus in a politically charged trap that could result in his arrest. Matthew shows how completely Jesus' contemporaries turned against him, to the degree that groups from opposite ends of the spectrum united in their schemes against him. The fierce tension between Jesus and the Pharisees emerges again in this account when Jesus calls them "hypocrites" before astounding them with an answer that cut through the political complexities of their time. Yet we should note that Jesus got involved in the important political and social issues of his time without aligning himself with a side. Jesus stayed committed to God's kingdom and worked for the purposes of God, providing an answer that rose above the disputes over taxes and religious allegiance.

Meanwhile, Luke presents a richer backstory to this encounter with the Jewish leaders. While he skips the technical names of each group, he reveals their motivations, fears, and ultimate hopes to hand Jesus over to the secular governor for trial. Luke's audience might not have been familiar with the details of Jesus' culture, so Luke points out that Jesus enjoyed popular support among the people, even if the Jewish leaders sought to kill him. Despite these differences, Luke keeps the general core of the story in place, as Jesus separates allegiance to government and worship of God.

As Jesus faces the trap set by the Pharisees and Herodians, he stands between the agendas of two groups. His message about God's present kingdom seems to hint at throwing off Roman rule, yet at the same time Jesus doesn't appear to be actively working against this occupying army. Depending on how he answered this question, Jesus risked trouble with either the Jews or the Romans.

Jesus' simple reply cuts to the heart of these leaders conspiring against him. They not only resented giving Caesar his financial dues, but they also held back the repentance and discipleship that God demands. While baptizing, John saw through the show of the Jewish leaders who didn't produce evidence of true repentance (Luke 3:7-9), and nothing has changed at this point in Jesus' ministry. Also, note that Matthew includes the detail that someone had to bring Jesus a Roman coin with the inscription of the occupying government. So Jesus seems to force his interrogators to squarely face the ugly reality of their nation, yet refuses them a completely clear answer.

At face value, Jesus tells them to obey the Romans. Yet he leaves some blanks for them to fill in: What should they really give to Caesar and what should they really give to God? And exactly where does the kingdom of God fit into Jesus' short but puzzling answer?

INSIGHTS FROM THE HISTORIC/GLOBAL CHURCH

Contemporary British scholar N. T. Wright occupies a significant space in New Testament scholarship both in the study of Jesus and in his writings on a new perspective of the apostle Paul. His thorough but readable study of Christian origins in *Jesus and the Victory of God* (Minneapolis, MN: Augsburg Fortress, 1997) adds fresh insights into the context of Jesus, and lends greater significance to the words of Christ that often fly by in a red-inked blur.

Wright digs into this conflict with Jesus and the Jewish leaders and casts Jesus' statement against the revolutionary overtones of Mattathias Maccabee, who said, "Pay back the Gentiles in full and obey the commands of the law" (1 Maccabees 2:68[3]). With this statement in mind, Wright shows that Jesus was making a revolutionary statement against compromise with Rome but also advocating cooperation with Rome to a certain extent because he didn't have a bloody revolt in mind.[4]

If this vague double-meaning has us scratching our heads, the second statement bears the same layering of meaning. Jesus clearly calls the Pharisees and Herodians to follow God with whole-hearted devotion, as each group compromised their faith in some way. But Wright carefully points to the significance of a coin bearing the image of a ruler—a ruler who no less claimed to be divine and might have even inscribed this on his coin—as a blatant blasphemy that the Pharisees would have found particularly galling;

this also explains the need to fetch a coin rather than simply pulling one out of their pockets.[5] Jesus might have been saying, if you have such a blasphemous coin around from this oppressive regime, just give it back to them. At the same time, Jesus prescribes joining God's present kingdom (rather than rebellion) as the solution. For, as Wright says, "The real rebellion would not come about through the non-payment of taxes and the resulting violent confrontation. It would be a matter of total obedience to, and imitation of, Israel's God; this would rule out violent revolution, as Matthew 5 makes clear."[6]

APPLYING TO MISSION

- Keeping in mind the idea of connecting our culture and theology, what do you see as the single greatest need in your community? What does the Bible say about this need?

- List two theological beliefs you hold that you think are important for your community.

- List three values that people in your community share. How do these cultural values affect the way you form theology?

LIVING OUT YOUR THEOLOGY

- What are some ways that Christians compromise when it comes to culture? How can we prevent this in the future?

- Go to a large bookstore (not a Christian one) and look through the Christian book section. Can you find one or more books that seem to incorrectly bring together Christian faith and today's culture? Discuss how these books have wedded theology and culture inappropriately. What can you do to avoid repeating their mistake?

Session 4

FROM MODERN TO POSTMODERN

To get the most out of this session,
I suggest reading chapters 4 and 5 in Coffeehouse Theology.

E ven if the words *modern* and *postmodern* rarely come up in a daily conversation, we can be certain that these two weighty philosophical movements have radically influenced much of our culture, and we should be sure we are clear on what these words mean.

As noted in *Coffeehouse Theology*, people in the modern age relied on individual reason, universal truth available to everyone, a direct correspondence between language and reality, and an orderly universe governed by laws. A key word to keep in mind with modernism is *reason*. Postmodernism refers to a period of time following the modern age when people took an interest in finding new perspectives to describe the world. Instead of seeking out a single story or perspective leading to one large and all-encompassing truth, thinkers began to value a diversity of perspectives and a collection of smaller, localized truths. In other words, we can define postmodernism as a rejection of larger truth for smaller truths—an embrace of complexity, chaos, and diversity.

These two systems of thought have seeped into popular culture, bringing changes in the areas of leadership, communication, entertainment, and certainly in the field of theology.

CONTEXT: MODERNISM VERSUS POSTMODERNISM

Most people who lived in the modern context assumed that knowledge can be 100 percent certain, that language largely corresponds with reality, and that the world is orderly and governed by laws. On the other hand, those native to postmodern thinking are fully aware of the subjective and local nature of knowledge, the ambiguity of language, and the inherent complexity and even chaos of our world.

While we don't need to have a master of philosophy degree or even know enough to explain these two philosophies for a class presentation, knowing a little about them can help us understand where we come from and how we can speak the truth of God prophetically in our world.[1] If our goal is to form and live out contextual theology, learning about these two contexts can help us better understand who we are today.

With this context in mind, ponder and discuss the following questions:

- Why do you think it's important to understand the eras or contexts referred to as modern and postmodern? How do you think these cultural lenses might affect our theology?

- What ways do you think the difference between modernism and postmodernism—particularly the idea of replacing a universal story with localized stories—might affect the way we present the gospel message?

- In what ways has modernism influenced culture today? How has postmodernism changed those influences?

- Write your own story about the collision of modern with post-modern, emphasizing the shift of seeing the world as orderly and governed to seeing it as complex and even chaotic. What do you think this means for Christians?

MEDITATION

Take some time to meditate on Acts 17:22-31 and then discuss the questions that follow:

> Paul then stood up in the meeting of the Areopagus and said: "Men of Athens! I see that in every way you are very religious. For as I walked around and looked carefully at your objects of worship, I even found an altar with this inscription: TO AN UNKNOWN GOD. Now what you worship as something unknown I am going to proclaim to you.
>
> "The God who made the world and everything in it is the Lord of heaven and earth and does not live in temples built by hands. And he is not served by human hands, as if he needed anything, because he himself gives all men life and breath and everything else. From one man he made every nation of men, that they should inhabit the whole earth; and he determined the times set for them and the exact places where they should live. God did this so that men would seek him and perhaps reach out for him and find him,

though he is not far from each one of us. 'For in him we live and move and have our being.' As some of your own poets have said, 'We are his offspring.'

"Therefore since we are God's offspring, we should not think that the divine being is like gold or silver or stone—an image made by man's design and skill. In the past God overlooked such ignorance, but now he commands all people everywhere to repent. For he has set a day when he will judge the world with justice by the man he has appointed. He has given proof of this to all men by raising him from the dead."

• How do you think Paul prepared for this speech?

• In what ways does Paul differentiate Christianity from the idolatry of the Greeks?

• What do Paul's references to the Greek poets add to his message?

• Summarize in your own words the gospel message at the end of Paul's speech.

- Read Acts 2 or Acts 7. How do the presentations of Peter and Stephen differ from Paul's speech in Acts 17?

MY THOUGHTS

Contemporary Christians who want to be culturally relevant in their ministries and sermons love Paul's famous sermon on Mars Hill. No other passage in Scripture so clearly demonstrates a creative and culturally appropriate message to a group outside of Judaism.

Rather than attacking the blatant idolatry that so vexed him, Paul begins his message with a compliment. After all, his Greek listeners set aside enormous amounts of time and money for their religious observances and monuments that still stand today. So Paul establishes common ground with them, because he and his audience are both committed to religion in some way. He exhibits this respect by walking around their religious areas to learn about them. Rather than hiding in the market, Paul makes an honest attempt to meet people where they are.

Paul's research pays off. Instead of saying, "I walked around your lousy idols and found them to be a waste of time," he establishes a key point of contact through the altar to an unknown god. Paul lets his hearers know their conscientious attention to every conceivable kind of god has paid off, and in fact they've already been worshipping this unknown god. Paul states that he will fill them in on the facts about this God so they can worship him properly.

Paul stresses that he's there to help, to give new information. For the Athenians, Paul offers the sweetest of candies, and it's an offer they can't refuse. And as he commends their worship rather than confronting or condemning them, Paul steers his speech toward the revealed truth of God, carefully holding the most troubling part until the very end.

As Paul continues, he keeps the Christian God grounded in familiar terms, stating that this God created the earth and everything in it. Then he carefully begins to depart from the Athenian religions. This God he proclaims has no use for temples, human servants, or statues, because the true God made everything, sustains it, and wants to know these people he sustains. In other words, God is very different from the Athenian gods because he not only has no need for fancy temples, he is closer and more personable than the Athenians could ever imagine. To make sure he keeps his audience, Paul even weaves in a connection with Athenian poets, proving that they've been pretty close to the truth all along.

Building on this idea of being "God's offspring," Paul moves into his conclusion that further differentiates God from Athenian idols. If the Greeks are willing to drop their erroneous religions, they can repent and enjoy a relationship with this personal God who nullifies idols and temples. And with this call to repentance in place, Paul presents the hard part: God will one day judge the world with justice—no longer overlooking naive idol worship[2]—and the resurrected Lord will be put in charge. At this point, Paul loses some of his audience, because the concept of a resurrection was laughably absurd in Jesus' day.[3] Still, Paul's careful planning pays off, as a few members of his audience follow along and agree to repent, while others at least seem willing to hear him again.

In the end, Paul provides a great example of one way to bring the gospel into a culture by demonstrating the need to establish common ground and then carefully point out both commonalities and differences, gradually working toward a culturally appropriate gospel presentation. Note that unlike Peter in Acts 2, Paul never mentions the Jewish origins of Jesus or his status as the Son of David. Paul skips the background and hits on the high points of the gospel about knowing God, repenting, and following him.

INSIGHTS FROM THE HISTORIC/GLOBAL CHURCH

American professor of theology and culture William Dyrness provides an impressive and accessible introduction to the helpful insights of global Christians in his book *Learning About Theology from the Third World*. As a middle-of-the-road corrective to missionaries who dismissed tribal religions of

Africa and those who closely blended African folk religion with Christianity, Dyrness describes the challenge for African Christians who relate to God within their established religious categories, but also reinterpret their world in light of the biblical witness. Dyrness looks directly to Paul in Acts 17 as his guide to this process:

> We have seen that most Africans believe that there is one who is creator and sustainer of all things. He is uniquely associated with the sky or the mountains, yet present at all times and places. In worship their deep sense of mystery and awe is pervasive. Is it true then, as Murorewa claims, that "African traditional religions provide African [Christian] theology with a theological framework in which the latter can develop" (1984:18)?
>
> Ordinarily missionaries did identify the God of the Bible with the high god of African religions. But this identification, while initially appropriate (compare Paul's strategy in Acts 17), should have led to a new scrutiny of the biblical record in the light of the African worldview.[4]

APPLYING TO MISSION

- How can we present truth in a postmodern context that sees complete objectivity as impossible? Is it necessary to consider new ways of living out the gospel message?

- What other potential pitfalls might the postmodern context hold for presenting the gospel?

COFFEEHOUSE THEOLOGY BIBLE STUDY GUIDE

- Given these pitfalls, how can your ministry or church adapt to effectively get out and share the gospel?

- What can we learn from African Christians about theology? In what ways do they fill in the sides of God we are unable to see?

LIVING OUT YOUR THEOLOGY

- Sketch a web of your own theological beliefs or doctrines. Place the most important ones in the middle and the less influential on the edges. Do your best to show how the beliefs relate to each other.

- List books, magazines, websites, movies, and any other part of our culture that can help us understand the values of our society and effectively form and share theology.

- Look into one of the resources you just listed and record your observations. What values do you see expressed? Where do you see common ground and where do you see differences from Christianity?

Session 5

CHRISTIANITY IN A CHANGING WORLD

To get the most out of this session,
I suggest reading chapter 6 in Coffeehouse Theology.

Brian McLaren—an author, speaker, pastor, and networker among Christian leaders, thinkers, and activists in the emerging church—stirred up a bit of controversy when he made the following statement: "You see, if we have a new world, we will need a new church."[1] Even if some regard McLaren's statement as imprecise, vague, and even a little troubling, he does bring up one of the most important issues Christians must wrestle with: How do we mesh faith and culture?

McLaren stands as one example of a Christian who is trying to follow Jesus in today's culture, taking to heart the words of theologian and minister Craig Van Gelder that no culturally pure expression of Christianity exists.[2] The modern world certainly brought changes to the church, ranging from wide availability of the Bible to the denominational splits we know today. All that we've inherited as members of the Christian faith has been shaped in some way by the modern age. We now face new challenges as the world shifts through postmodernism and its emphasis on diversity and complexity.

Christians in this context will need to hold to the truth passed down through our history and found in conversations with global Christians, commit to humbly reading and rereading Scripture, and always cling to the simple truth that God holds the truth and sustains our world.

CONTEXT: A WHOLE NEW WORLD

Perhaps the world hasn't changed to the degree that we have "a whole new world," carpet rides with Aladdin aside. However, philosophical shifts and technical advances have reshaped many parts of contemporary culture. The Christian faith can't exist apart from a cultural context. And because context will work its influence one way or another, we might as well face the challenge of contextual theology now, rather than finding out that undetected elements in our surrounding culture have skewed our theological conclusions.

A "new church" or "new kind of Christian" might overstate the ways Christians should respond to today's culture. However, there's no doubt the church has changed before in the face of society's shifts, and it will once again need to change to some degree.

With this context in mind, ponder and discuss the following questions:

- How can Christians balance certainty with the leap required by faith? How does Christianity speak to the pluralism and diversity of today's culture?

- What ways have you observed the culture changing the church? Which of these ways are you comfortable with? Which makes you most uncomfortable? Explain.

- Look up some information on the emerging church. What value does the emerging church hold for theologians today?

- How does the meshing of faith and culture change your approach to theology?

MEDITATION

Take some time to meditate on Colossians 1:10-14[3]:

> And we pray this in order that you may live a life worthy of the Lord and may please him in every way: bearing fruit in every good work, growing in the knowledge of God, being strengthened with all power according to his glorious might so that you may have great endurance and patience, and joyfully giving thanks to the Father, who has qualified you to share in the inheritance of the saints in the kingdom of light. For he has rescued us from the dominion of darkness and brought us into the kingdom of the Son he loves, in whom we have redemption, the forgiveness of sins.

MY THOUGHTS

In the margin of my NIV Thinline Bible, next to the text of Romans 1, I scrawled, "We are debtors." I didn't quite see the connection to the passage, but the guest preacher that Sunday seemed pretty hot on the theme, returning to it over and over again. My cousin (eleven years old at the time) happened to be visiting that Sunday, and it was the first time he'd heard a fired-up Baptist preacher—he later confessed to being quite afraid. I'm guessing now that the preacher was probably camped out in Romans 1:18-20. But as a teen-ager, I struggled with tuning in for a lecture. This kind of sermon outlining human sin, our failure to meet God's standards, and the subsequent need for the death of Jesus to satisfy God's righteous demands was fairly typical for the fundamentalist Baptist church I attended in my early years as a follower of Jesus.

The summary of this salvation narrative runs like this: God has a holy law that humans have violated. God can't tolerate sin, so humanity is on the outs with God. God sends his Son to die in our place and to satisfy the demands of his righteous laws.

This concept of owing a debt to God gained tremendous traction in Protestant circles, especially among the theologically conservative. While the Old Testament is filled with animal sacrifices and offerings for sins, Jesus fulfilled that entire system through his death and resurrection. This means that cows, sheep, bulls, and doves can all breathe a collective sigh of relief. But for all of its popularity, perhaps the story of salvation is more complicated than we've thought.

Paul writes to the Colossians to confront a false teaching that blended elements of Judaism and Greek philosophy that added unnecessary practices and challenged the supremacy of Christ. In Colossians 2, Paul gets to the heart of his argument that because of Christ's completeness as true God, the Colossian Christians can rest assured they are spiritually complete in him, and they can ignore false teachers who try to add burdens to the freedom of the gospel.

While he's at it, Paul makes an important statement that Christ "is the head over every power and authority." In other words, not only does Jesus save his people from the condemnation of God, he has conquered the powers of this world. While this element in the story of salvation receives little airtime in many Christian circles, Paul lists it as the key reason why he can pray for the growth, strength, and joy of the church.

Paul's prayer provides a great example of putting theology into practice. He uses the spiritual reality of God's redemption to pray for the continued

endurance and blessing of the Colossian Christians. He ties their qualifica-
tion into the inheritance of the saints and God's kingdom to their rescue
by God from the dominion of darkness. As many other Scripture passages
suggest, a spiritual battle pits the servants of God against the servants of
darkness or Satan. Paul enlarges the scope of this struggle that can appear
on a day to day basis (see Ephesians 6:12) to encompass the entire story of
redemption. Instead of paying a debt to himself in order to satisfy his righteous demands, God is shown as the rescuer from sin and the kingdom of
darkness that opposes his rule.

In addition, the death and resurrection of Christ once and for all defeated
these powers of darkness, establishing Christ as the victor (*Christus Victor*)
over all principalities and powers. This expanded conception of redemption
has proven helpful for many theologians as they share the gospel.

A pastor I know counsels people who have endured abuse. One day he
began to share the gospel with a young woman, explaining how humanity
falls short of the standards of the holy and righteous God. In order to save
people from sin and make them acceptable in his sight, God sent his only
Son to die for them, paying their debt to God and paving the way for them
to have eternal life.

Although this story has been told thousands upon thousands of times
and has led many to understand and accept the mercy and sacrifice of God
(including myself), this young woman was revolted. To the surprise of the
pastor, the young woman, who had suffered abuse in her past, said, "You've
just described God as a cosmic child abuser." Instead of bowing her head
and praying to accept Christ, she said, "No thanks—that's one messed up
God."

The trouble here is that this simple summary of salvation is basically true.
People are separated from God by sin and God does make his standards for
holiness and obedience clear throughout Scripture. Sin is certainly a problem, and Jesus is definitely the solution. But who really keeps people away
from God? Are God's standards really the problem? Can we discover a way
to understand salvation that doesn't make God into a villain or "cosmic child
abuser" who sacrificed his Son on a cross?

Understanding Christ as victor in Colossians 1:13-14 won't solve all of our problems in sharing the gospel. But to a world that views God with suspicion as a vengeful and angry punisher of sinners, we need to be willing to take other facets of Christian revelation into account. While the doctrine of Christus Victor shouldn't replace the legal concept of salvation where Jesus accepts the penalty for our sins, we can gain rich insights into salvation through this view of salvation that emerged in the early church and that several contemporary theologians have brought back into the spotlight.[4]

INSIGHTS FROM THE HISTORIC/GLOBAL CHURCH

The church father Irenaeus was an early proponent of the ransom view of atonement that is closely tied with Christus Victor, as Christ ransoms fallen humanity from the grip of Satan. Irenaeus emphasized that Christ did not use force to accomplish this but sacrificed himself as the means of persuading the enemy. C. S. Lewis takes a similar approach in *The Lion, the Witch, and the Wardrobe* with Aslan's sacrifice. (In the following excerpt, it helps to know that Jesus is the "Word," while Satan is the "apostate one".) Irenaus wrote:

> Thus the powerful Word and true human being, ransoming us by his own blood in a rational manner, gave himself as a ransom for those who have been led into captivity. The apostate one unjustly held sway over us, and though we were by nature the possession of Almighty God, we have been alienated from our proper nature, making us instead his own disciples. Therefore the almighty Word of God, who did not lack justice, acted justly even in the encounter with the apostate one, ransoming from him the things which were his own, but not by force, in the way in which [the apostate one] secured his own dominion over us at the beginning, by greedily snatching what was not his own. Rather, it was appropriate that God should obtain what he wished through persuasion, not by the use of force, so that the principles of justice might not be infringed, and, at the same time, that God's original creation might not perish.[5]

APPLYING TO MISSION

- In Colossians 1:10-14, what does the phrase "dominion of darkness" refer to? How does our rescue from the dominion of darkness change our everyday lives?

- How can expanding the story of salvation to include "Christ as the Victor" change the way you share the gospel and minister? Do you believe this metaphor works in the postmodern context? Explain.

- Look into a modern Christian organization fighting a modern-day slave trade, such as Stop the Traffik or Not for Sale. What biblical basis do these groups have for their work? How does the message of Christus Victor apply to such ministries?

LIVING OUT YOUR THEOLOGY

- View the movie versions of *Godspell* or *Jesus Christ Superstar*. How are these representations of Jesus products of their time? How does our current context affect our perspectives of Jesus?

- How can we balance Christus Victor with the legal/substitution view of salvation that many Christians have followed for the past five hundred years?

Session 6

THE FIRST AND ONLY FOUNDATION

To get the most out of this session,
I suggest reading chapter 7 in Coffeehouse Theology.

If theology is the study of God, and if we have no hope of knowing God apart from what he reveals to us, then maybe it makes good sense to start out with God himself as the center of theology.

Of course, in a practical way, the trouble we often face is that we don't know where to place God in our study. For starters, God reaches out to us and makes it possible to follow him—every Christian arrives at salvation because God took the first step. The Holy Spirit is also behind our study of Scripture, illuminating the truth as we dig into the message and helping us apply it to our lives as we meditate on biblical texts. Still, many Christians place Scripture at the forefront of theological reflection. Because we don't really understand exactly how divine revelation works, we find it difficult to reserve a place for God at the start of our study.

Our challenge is to hear God's voice and follow the Spirit's lead in our interpretations without collapsing into some subjective spiritual melee where every Christian claims to have a direct revelation from God. The key is doing theology in Christian community where we can observe the work of God and check our interpretations against Scripture, tradition, and the global church.

Yes, Scripture might well be the first source we turn to when we study God, but our study of Scripture depends on the revelation of God's Spirit. That's why we need to recognize that God comes above everything else, even the very Word that reveals him to us.

CONTEXT: PUTTING GOD FIRST

As Christians living in the postmodern context, we have opportunities and challenges. On the opportunity side, we find people more open to a diversity of perspectives and even willing to include religion as an important part of their lives again.[1] Still, with the importance of diversity, many are offended by any belief system that claims to be the only way. And even if "religion" is popular, the basic Christian knowledge held by our culture has waned.[2] As Christians, then, our challenge is to learn about God and to share the gospel in a context where we assume that even if our listeners are interested in spirituality, they don't have a basic understanding of the Judeo-Christian God. At the same time, we need to remember that the people we're speaking to aren't closed off to the idea of God or even Jesus.[3]

When we talk about God, we face the challenge of explaining the faith anew to people who know little about the Christian God, and may need to be challenged in their tendency to blend the concepts of various spiritual movements. This tendency is known as syncretism. I've had many conversations in which I explain a doctrinally sound characteristic of God and the individual agrees with me. Yet in the same conversation, he then speaks of reincarnation or some other mystical belief as equally valid.

Sometimes it is harder to explain the Christian God to someone who accepts a conglomeration of beliefs about God than to someone who simply doubts or denies God's existence completely. Regardless of what the people we talk to believe about God, in many conversations we'll hear a response like this: "I'm glad you've found God and that works for you. I'm very religious but in my own way."

While we can debate the point sometimes, it's often best to simply let the conversation rest and leave the door open for further dialogue. As Christians, we need to remember that we have a solid foundation for life in Christ himself, and should therefore make it our chief business to live in this truth, allowing God's Spirit to rule in our lives. Then, when the self-constructed religious beliefs of others fall to pieces in the grind of life, we can gently and lovingly deliver the wonderful news that the Lord over all is deeply interested in them.

With this context in mind, ponder and discuss the following questions:

- If we begin theology with God, how does that change our approach to the Bible?

- As Christians, how should we respond to postmodern philosophers who claim there is no absolute truth?

- How does syncretism today make it a challenge to share the message of the gospel? How do you think Christians should deal with it?

MEDITATION

Take some time to meditate on 1 Corinthians 3:10-13 and then discuss the questions that follow:

By the grace God has given me, I laid a foundation as an expert builder, and someone else is building on it. But each one should be careful how he builds. For no one can lay any foundation other than the one already laid, which is Jesus Christ. If any man builds on this foundation using gold, silver, costly stones, wood, hay or straw, his work will be shown for what it is, because the Day will bring it to light. It will be revealed with fire, and the fire will test the quality of each man's work.

- What things might Christians mistakenly use as a foundation other than Jesus?

- Paul lists a number of building materials. What do you think each of these symbolizes?

MY THOUGHTS

Christians in the United States often evaluate the success of their churches by taking a head count. The brochures of Christian conferences typically boast the number of members in each speaker's church. I've been in small churches that have leveled off numerically, where we almost panted at the thought of one, two, or three thousand members, envying megachurches that had figured out the secret to attracting a large number of people. And when we studied these churches, hoping to unlock the mystery of higher attendance, we inevitably found some startling answers.

Some leaders pointed to a clear vision statement, others relied on small groups, while others said they hired top notch musicians for their Sunday services. The pastor of a large church in northern New Jersey provided one of the most jarring answers: "We preach the gospel."

Wow—there must be more to church than just preaching the gospel! But the foundation of every Christian community must be the message that Jesus, the crucified and risen Savior, is Lord and brings the life of God to us today. Clever social tools and plans can follow, but at the center—at the very foundation—we must find Jesus.

Some churches can trace their success either to celebrity preachers or excellent management of social groups. Of course, many faithfully preach the gospel as well. But it's also possible to have a large church and a weak or even nonexistent gospel. And even if the preaching of many churches comes straight from the Bible, some owe their allegiance more to certain preachers or denominational lines rather than simply relying on Christ. It's an easy mistake to make.

While Paul is the be-all, end-all for many Christians today,[4] in his own times he wasn't exactly in high demand. As a preacher he was timid and uninspiring. Some churches refused to support him and instead sent their money after far more eloquent and impressive preachers. However, God's power and authority distinguished Paul from the popular preachers of Corinth. In 1 Corinthians 2:2-4, Paul claims that he relied wholly on the message of Jesus Christ crucified and the power of the Spirit. Management prowess, fame, and denominational affiliation didn't enter the equation. In fact, Paul rebukes the Corinthians for identifying with Christian leaders instead of Christ himself.

Paul cut through the quarrels of this immature church by pointing them to Christ and Christ alone as the starting point for the church. He reminded them that it didn't matter who preached the first message or baptized the believers. Instead, Paul instructed the Corinthian Christians to find their unity in Christ, the foundation of the church.

Paul echoes Jesus' warning to the teachers of the Jewish law, urging the Corinthian Christians to avoid falling into the same trap: "You diligently study the Scriptures because you think that by them you possess eternal life. These are the Scriptures that testify about me, yet you refuse to come to me to have life" (John 5:39-40). Even if someone tries to displace Christ, Paul makes it clear that Christ is the foundation for the people of God. When God brings this world under scrutiny at the end of this age, only those who base their lives on Christ will have something permanent and secure.

INSIGHTS FROM THE HISTORIC/GLOBAL CHURCH

In his comprehensive treatment of the Resurrection, British theologian
N. T. Wright believes that 1 Corinthians 3:10-15 powerfully illuminates the
continuity and discontinuity between our present world and the coming age
under God's rule.

> Nowhere else do we have such a strong sense of the continuity,
> across the moment of fiery judgment, between the work done in the
> present and the new world that the Creator God intends to make.
> Well-built houses, says Paul, will last; they will, in other words, be
> part of the coming world the creator intends. Good, faithful apos-
> tolic work, whether in the foundation-laying or in the building, will
> last. . . . Once again, Paul is longing for the Corinthians to under-
> stand themselves, the church and the work of their teachers within
> an eschatological narrative, a story which runs from the present
> age to the age to come, with church and apostle alike poised in the
> tense overlap between the two. . . .
>
> Paul believes that with the resurrection of the Messiah the new
> world has already begun; that the Spirit comes from that future
> into the present, to shape, prepare and enable people and churches
> for that future; and the work done in the power of the Spirit in the
> present will therefore last into the future.[5]

APPLYING TO MISSION

- How do Wright's insights change your perspective on your ministry
  or the ministry you hope to carry out some day?

- Wright says, "The work done in the power of the Spirit in the present will therefore last into the future." How do we distinguish between work done in the power of the Spirit and work that is not?

LIVING OUT YOUR THEOLOGY

- Evaluate the risks and benefits of beginning theology with God at the center.

- Read John 16. Describe the relationship between God and Scripture.

- When should Christians try to explain God and when should they let the mystery of God stand? Explain.

THE BIBLE: OUR SALVATION STORY

To get the most out of this session,
I suggest reading chapter 8 in Coffeehouse Theology.

Along with the revelation of God, Scripture lies at the center of Christian theology. The early church recognized the unique character of these documents, which are closely linked with the apostles of Christ, giving them a primary place over other documents that carried spiritual benefits.

Throughout Christian history, church leaders have debated the place of church tradition alongside Scripture. But even if some Christians don't strictly adhere to the Protestant rallying cry *sola Scriptura* (Scripture alone), no follower of Christ denies the authority and centrality of Scripture. Rather than providing an instruction manual on how exactly to live, Scripture acts as a portrait that illustrates how God interacts with people and works to bring salvation. The Bible is a representation of how God works in our world, but it's not the only story or even the end of the story.

The narrative of the Bible doesn't instruct all followers of God for all times exactly how to worship or how to live a holy life. These details change over time. Christians bear the important role of interpreters who take the histories, poems, oracles, and letters of Scripture and determine how to live as God's people today. While listening to the Holy Spirit, Christian tradition, and global Christians, Christian theologians—and by theologian, I mean anyone who follows Christ—turn to Scripture as the norm for our walks with God and the ethics we practice on earth. Scripture is our primary source when learning about God.

CONTEXT: THE BIBLE IN POSTMODERN CULTURE

A wide range of perspectives about the Bible exist in the denominations and traditions of churches in the United States. Catholics and Eastern Orthodox Christians read Scripture with a heavy emphasis on traditions, while many Protestants are suspicious of tradition. Even when Protestants do mention traditions, they tend to focus on events that have happened since the dawn of the Protestant Reformation. All groups say the Bible is important, but we have yet to agree on a way to balance the Bible with all of the traditions passed down to us.

And then, as we press into contextual theology, we have the matter of mixing our findings of Scripture with today's culture. Within the Protestant camp, some attempt to adhere to a "plain" (or common sense) reading of what the Bible means, separating themselves from culture and trying to remain true to the self-evident teachings of Scripture. Others occupy a middle ground, trying to balance Christianity and culture with varying degrees of success. And still others have allowed modern categories to determine how they read the Bible, ruling out miracles and other divine elements of the faith in order to focus on the mission of Jesus as servant to humanity.[1] Finally, other groups try to preserve the historic Christian faith, while also working within the norms and categories of culture to one degree or another. So we all agree that the Bible is important, we just can't agree on how to include culture in the mix.

In the midst of these complexities among denominations and culture, there's no shortage of opinions on how to read the Bible or how to uncover the cultural setting of Scripture. In fact, we typically spend far more time talking about the world of the Bible than our own traditions or context and how they influence the way we read Scripture.

Walk into any bookstore with a Christianity section and you'll find all kinds of dubious books claiming to uncover the "real" Jesus or explaining some new element of Christianity that a certain scholar uncovered in some mystery cult and that sheds fresh light on the setting of the Bible. Orthodox Christian scholars also work hard to uncover the ancient world of Scripture in commentaries, dictionaries, and various other books explaining elements of the biblical world. Many even break new ground by reexamining the Bible in light of Judaism from the time of Christ. And with all of this information we've accumulated about the Bible, we forget that culture comes into play in two ways: the writers of the biblical books in their day and the readers today.

That's where the postmodern context enters into our conversation. On one level, the postmodern context hints that our culture influences how we read the Bible and that we desperately need to include perspectives outside our own. At the same time, the postmodern context causes a problem when it also hints that we'll never find any solid truth to trust in. Our challenge today is to balance our knowledge of the biblical world with our own because both influence our interpretations and ultimately determine how we'll follow Jesus.

With this context in mind, ponder and discuss the following questions:

- What's your denomination's view on the Bible and general method of interpreting it? If you don't know, this is a good time to find out. What do you see as the strengths and weaknesses of this view? Consider asking someone from another denomination to work on this question with you.

- Compare and contrast the metaphors of Scripture as a blueprint versus Scripture as a painting.

- How does the postmodern context affect the way we read the Bible?

- What are the opportunities and challenges we face when reading the Bible in the postmodern context?

MEDITATION

Take some time to meditate on Acts 2:32-36 and Psalm 110:1-2 and then discuss the questions that follow:

God has raised this Jesus to life, and we are all witnesses of the fact. Exalted to the right hand of God, he has received from the Father the promised Holy Spirit and has poured out what you now see and hear. For David did not ascend to heaven, and yet he said,

"The Lord said to my Lord:
'Sit at my right hand
until I make your enemies
a footstool for your feet.'"

Therefore let all Israel be assured of this: God has made this Jesus, whom you crucified, both Lord and Christ. (Acts 2:32-36)

The LORD says to my Lord:
"Sit at my right hand

until I make your enemies
    a footstool for your feet."

The LORD will extend your mighty scepter from Zion;
    You will rule in the midst of your enemies. (Psalm 110:1-2)

- Look up and read all of Psalm 110. Compare what you think the author originally intended to say with what Peter says in Acts 2.

- Who is "my Lord" in these passages?

MY THOUGHTS

In a book filled with stories about Paul getting beat up, chased out of town, shipwrecked, and even bitten by a snake, we can easily overlook Peter's powerful sermon that jumpstarted the church. Paul preaches in Athens, escapes in a basket over a wall, and is even mistaken for a god. That's quite a list of stories to share around the campfire!

Poor Peter.

You'd wonder what he really did in the early church (unless perhaps you're a Catholic) when you compare the amount of airtime he receives compared to Paul. Still, Peter holds center stage early on in Acts as he presents the story of the risen Christ to an assortment of Jews, complete with numerous biblical references to the pouring out of God's Spirit under the rule of his Son, the heir of David and the Messiah.

A modern interpreter might wonder how Peter won over his listeners so quickly with his loosely connected string of Scriptures. The two psalms of David he quotes (see Acts 2:25-28,34-35) contain no reference to a Messiah, no reference to the Crucifixion, and maybe a vague reference to the Resurrection. Why did Peter include these psalms? Why did his listeners believe Jesus is the Lord? And why did they respond with repentance and baptism?

Although Peter might be described as a theological amateur, he still knew his Scripture and the traditions surrounding it. At best, Psalm 110 is hard for us to sort out. In most English translations the small-caps LORD (YHWH) and David's Lord hold a conversation of sorts. But who is David's Lord?

One tradition in the Judaism of Peter's day believed this *Lord* referred to the Messiah—the one who will come to establish God's kingdom. Jesus himself picked up on this tradition (see Matthew 22:41-46) when he questioned the Pharisees about the Son of David, a messianic title (see Mark 10:47). We might interpret it this way: The Lord of David is greater than David himself, but different in some way from the LORD.[2] During the period between the Old Testament era and the start of the New Testament era, the title "Son of David" became meshed with the concept of a Messiah. In fact, Psalm 110 emerged as one of the primary texts supporting this claim of Davidic and messianic kingship.

Peter points to the manifestation of the Holy Spirit among those present as proof that something significant has happened in salvation history: Jesus has proven his status as Lord over all by conquering all of his enemies, even death, and proclaiming victory by pouring out the Spirit of God. Even David, with his temporary and imperfect rule, didn't ascend to heaven. But Jesus, now sitting at God's right hand, has established himself as the Messiah and Lord over all. A cosmic spiritual shift has taken place as God has sent his Spirit into what was previously considered enemy territory. Peter presents the supremacy of the risen Lord who fulfills and surpasses David as the reason behind the wonderful events of Pentecost morning. Recognizing the unexpected fulfillment of prophecy, Peter's listeners respond to the move of God and message of Jesus' messianic rule.

Peter knew his audience and their common understanding of traditions related to the coming of the Messiah. He used his religious traditions and the common understanding of the Messiah to clearly communicate who Jesus is. Peter no doubt used Scripture to make his point, but without an understanding of his times and the biblical traditions of the people at this time, we'd find it difficult to figure out his line of reasoning. Peter's sensitivity to context and careful use of Scripture and tradition show us one way of communicating the revelation of God.

INSIGHTS FROM THE HISTORIC/GLOBAL CHURCH

Lesslie Newbigin left his native Britain to serve as a missionary in India in 1936. After nearly forty years as a minister and bishop, Newbigin returned home to retire but soon became active through lecturing, pastoring, and penning two masterful works on the gospel and culture: *Foolishness to the Greeks: The Gospel and Western Culture* (Grand Rapids, MI: Eerdmans, 1986) and *The Gospel in a Pluralist Society* (Grand Rapids, MI: Eerdmans, 1989). Newbigin was influential in the establishment of the Gospel and Our Culture network, as well as revolutionizing the way the church thinks of interacting with culture. His forty years abroad and brilliant work as a scholar make him one of the most important voices in the fields of theology and missiology—a field tied directly to contextual theology.

In *The Gospel in a Pluralist Society*, Newbigin addresses the mission of the church and the fact that most gospel proclamations in the New Testament are in response to a question from an outsider:

> The answer of Peter is in effect a statement that what is going on is that the last day has arrived and the power of the new age is already at work, and that this is so because of the life, ministry, death, resurrection, and ascension of Jesus. The sermon leads up to a climax in the citing of Psalm 110 (Acts 2:34). Jesus, whom they had crucified, is now seated at the right hand of God until all things are put under his feet.[3]

Newbigin is pointing to the fact that the mission of the kingdom belongs to God, who has initiated a new age. The Spirit takes the initiative, and then the disciples of Christ move in where God is at work. It is not the work of the church to save the world, but rather to join God as he saves the world. There is still a place for preaching the gospel, but the initiative belongs to God.

APPLYING TO MISSION

- Can you recall times when you sensed the Holy Spirit taking the initiative in an area of ministry? How did you know this was the work of the Spirit? How did you respond?

- How can we balance preparing for ministry with leaving the initiative up to God?

LIVING OUT YOUR THEOLOGY

- Does your denomination or tradition gravitate to a particular book or genre of the Bible? If you answered yes, why do you think this takes place?

- Review Galatians 4 and Acts 2. Did Paul and Peter correctly apply the Old Testament passages they referenced? What did they do differently from theologians today?

- Take a look at a chapter of Scripture you've read recently and list some connections between the message of that passage and our culture today.

- In *Coffeehouse Theology* I list some online resources you can use in your study of the Bible. Choose three websites from www.zoecarnate .com and spend five minutes reviewing each of them.

Session 8

LEARNING FROM OUR TRADITIONS

To get the most out of this session,
I suggest reading chapter 9 in Coffeehouse Theology.

While we often overlook the history of the church, it can serve as one of our greatest resources for doing theology. Having endured plagues, wars, and heresies, the traditions accumulated throughout church history are responsible for what we believe today.

Still, even with this rich tradition behind us, some of our doctrines result from theology's interaction with our contemporary situation, and we should scrutinize these tenets to a greater degree. For example, in *The Civil War as a Theological Crisis* (Chapel Hill, NC: University of North Carolina Press, 2006), author Mark Knoll skillfully describes the American Civil War (1861–1865) in terms of a theological conflict that pitted Northern theologians against Southern theologians, each committed to biblical interpretations that backed up their lifestyles and politics. In addition, each side wrestled with divine providence while trying to determine what exactly God intended to do through the events of the times. Knoll reveals how the context of each side colored their views of Scripture and added kindling to the controversies at the heart of the war.

Whether we like it or not, our traditions already play a major role in our theological beliefs. As divided and troubled as it might be, we really have no other Christianity than the one passed down to us. Because we can't ignore or escape our traditions, the most logical solution is to work on understanding them and how they shape who we are. We can even use this history to great advantage by learning about mistakes and triumphs of the past—attempting to learn from the mistakes and building on what has stood the test of time.

CONTEXT: THE VALUE OF CHRISTIAN HISTORY TODAY

History does pretty well in the United States. Historical documentaries and nonfiction narratives regularly stir up a great deal of public interest, providing historical facts in small and easily digested chunks. Historians such as David McCullough have zoomed in on historical giants such as John Adams and Harry Truman, not to mention his best-selling narrative *1776*. In 2007, Ken Burns captivated audiences with his long-awaited documentary on World War II, aptly named *The War*.

The church hasn't always followed where popular culture has gone, and that's a problem in this case. Although many excellent books on Christian history do exist, many churches have dumped the role of history in their *sola Scriptura* (Scripture alone) approach to theology. In reality, many Christians know precious little about Christian history.

With this context in mind, ponder and discuss the following questions:

- Where does tradition fit into your theological beliefs? Why?

- How should Christians use tradition when forming theology?

- In session 6, I defined syncretism as blending the concepts of Christian faith with other spiritual influences. How does Christian tradition help guard against syncretism?

MEDITATION

Take some time to meditate on Matthew 12:1-8.

> At that time Jesus went through the grainfields on the Sabbath. His disciples were hungry and began to pick some heads of grain and eat them. When the Pharisees saw this, they said to him, "Look! Your disciples are doing what is unlawful on the Sabbath."
>
> He answered, "Haven't you read what David did when he and his companions were hungry? He entered the house of God, and he and his companions ate the consecrated bread—which was not lawful for them to do, but only for the priests. Or haven't you read in the Law that on the Sabbath the priests in the temple desecrate the day and yet are innocent? I tell you that one greater than the temple is here. If you had known what these words mean, 'I desire mercy, not sacrifice,' you would not have condemned the innocent. For the Son of Man is Lord of the Sabbath."

MY THOUGHTS

Jesus and the Jews of his day had a slight advantage over Christians today. Except for the roughly one hundred years of writings that have become the New Testament, our traditions aren't canonized into an authoritative collection. However, the most important traditions of the Jews appeared in the historic and prophetic books, meaning Jesus could quote from the Torah (Genesis through Deuteronomy), and he could also quote Scripture verses concerning the way later generations of Jewish teachers interpreted these texts in the Wisdom Literature and the Prophets. These later Scriptures provided a helpful guide in applying the older texts to new contexts.

In this encounter with the Pharisees, Jesus refers to Exodus and Leviticus, but also sharpens his focus by quoting from 1 Samuel and the prophet Hosea. This rich interpretive tradition reveals a God who isn't set in his ways about laws. In fact, he's willing to make exceptions to the law.

From the standpoint of the Pharisees, Exodus 23:12 and Leviticus 23:3 couldn't be clearer. What part of "priests only" did Jesus not understand? So Jesus throws the story of David back at them, asking, "What part of 1 Samuel 21:6 don't you understand?" Jesus then tacks on a reference to the work of the priests on the Sabbath day and the words of God in Hosea 6:6 regarding God's preference for mercy over sacrifice. In the space of a few verses recorded by Matthew, Jesus stacks up biblical support to contradict the Scripture verses the Jewish teachers rallied to their cause.

The Pharisees had developed nitpicky and over-the-top interpretations of Scripture, and they often went to extreme lengths to pursue legal purity. But by referencing David and Hosea, Jesus goes straight to the heart of the Pharisees' problem: They had created a religious system that ignored the complexities of Scripture and that also ignored God's greater concerns for mercy. By overlooking the traditions and stories that didn't line up with the narrative they'd constructed, the Jewish teachers suppressed the larger story of God. As a result, they didn't recognize the incarnate God when he spoke with them directly.

INSIGHTS FROM THE HISTORIC/GLOBAL CHURCH

American theologian Richard B. Hayes has written extensively on the New Testament and biblical interpretation. In his comprehensive and accessible study of New Testament ethics, *The Moral Vision of the New Testament* (San Francisco: HarperSanFrancisco, 1996), Hayes finds some startling implications in the related passages of Matthew 9:13 and 12:7 that bear the common thread of Jesus quoting Hosea 6:6.

The christological [sic] claim that Jesus is greater than the Temple and that therefore those who serve him are, like priests in the Temple, not subject to the ordinary requirements on Sabbath activity is an extraordinarily bold—some would say nearly blasphemous—assertion; in the aftermath of the temple's destruction, it takes on a specially freighted import. To this christological [sic] argument is coupled once again an appeal to the Hosea text: the "hermeneutic of mercy" supplants or relativizes the Law's specific commandments (cf. Exod. 34:21).

In these passages we see the outworking of Matthew's earlier claim in the Sermon on the Mount that Jesus fulfills rather than negates the Law. When that formula is applied to test cases, such as eating with sinners and harvesting grain on the Sabbath, we see that the Law is understood to bear witness to what Matthew elsewhere calls "the weightier matters of the law: justice and mercy and faith" (23:23). Jesus' teaching provides a dramatic new hermeneutical filter that necessitates a rereading of everything in the Law in light of the dominant imperative of mercy.[1]

APPLYING TO MISSION

- Research your own denomination's or tradition's history. Where has it been successful? When has it failed?

- Look up a Christian creed or confession (try www.carm.org/creeds .htm). What does it teach you about the roots of your beliefs?

LIVING OUT YOUR THEOLOGY

- List at least three ways you can integrate Christian tradition into your theology.

- Choose one and spend fifteen to thirty minutes this week putting it into practice.

- Have a conversation with (or look up a blog by) someone from a different denomination and find out about the historic roots of their beliefs. In what ways does their history affect these beliefs? What beliefs differ from your own?

Session 9

THE DIVERSITY OF THE CHURCH

To get the most out of this session,
I suggest reading chapter 10 in Coffeehouse Theology.

Theology isn't supposed to be a lonely task. With theologians dotted across every continent, missionaries sharing stories of God at work abroad, denominations bringing rich traditions, and the variety of believers in local churches, we have many partners available for the growth of a robust and diverse dialogue. As we become aware of our own cultural limitations, these voices outside our own context provide fresh perspectives that lead to a clearer picture of the truth, even if we end up seeing a muddle of different interpretations and readings until we sort them all out.

As we form theology, we can never give in to subjectivity or relativism. Yet we can accept a certain level of complexity to our world that should lead us to remain humble and dependent on the insights of our Christian brothers and sisters in other cultures. Otherwise, we run the risk of establishing our own culture as the authoritative norm for all times and all people.

CONTEXT: THE WORLD AT OUR DOOR

Thanks to the Internet and the growth of global trade, we find our world more interconnected than ever. We can read about democracy activists in Burma (also known as Myanmar), the opinions of Iranian bloggers, and the mess of war and genocide in certain African nations. And at the same time, we can also catch up on news about the latest commercial development in our city or victories by our local sports teams. What's more, American companies claim that jobs outsourced to Eastern nations such as India and China help keep costs down, while the same countries and others ship cheap products west for American consumers demanding the lowest prices (for better or worse).

As everything in our world becomes more interconnected and spread around the globe, many local markets in other countries suffer. Global markets have raised the price of food and other goods so that the average person in small villages can barely afford to eat. Meanwhile the interiors of American towns lose their local mom-and-pop businesses in favor of large box stores that sell cheaper imports sprouting on the city limits.

This global interdependence and awareness hasn't yet translated into a cohesive global theological trend that the majority of Christians in America recognize. Most of us aren't used to listening to global Christian voices. Our reliance on our own objectivity and the Bible alone give rise to theologies that not only pay little attention to Christians throughout the world but also exhibit a disconcerting self-confidence. And while some churches are aware of Christians suffering in other lands or facing difficult social and economic circumstances, most of us don't realize how much these believers on other continents have to teach us.

Thankfully, this is beginning to change. Books, articles,[1] and blogs celebrate the unique perspectives offered by Latin American, Asian, African, and Eastern European theologians, providing new avenues for biblical study that most of us haven't yet tried. While our churches rightly cling to their unique identities and perspectives, we also have an opportunity to use the availability of information through the Internet and other resources to open a theological conversation with the global church. This represents a welcome addition to theology in a postmodern world where multiple perspectives provide helpful guides to truth.

With this context in mind, ponder and discuss the following questions:

- How do theologians from a variety of denominations help theology? Do they hinder it in any way?

- What are the benefits of including global theologians in our reflections on God?

- Have you ever been surprised by the views of someone from another part of the world? Explain.

- Can you think of ways you've listened to global voices in order to form and act out your beliefs? What about times you've ignored these voices from other cultures? Explain.

MEDITATION

Take some time to meditate on Genesis 11:1-9 and then discuss the questions that follow:

> Now the whole world had one language and a common speech. As men moved eastward, they found a plain in Shinar and settled there.
>
> They said to each other, "Come, let's make bricks and bake them thoroughly." They used brick instead of stone, and tar for mortar. Then they said, "Come, let us build ourselves a city, with a tower that reaches to the heavens, so that we may make a name for ourselves and not be scattered over the face of the whole earth."
>
> But the LORD came down to see the city and the tower that the men were building. The LORD said, "If as one people speaking the same language they have begun to do this, then nothing they plan to do will be impossible for them. Come, let us go down and confuse their language so they will not understand each other."
>
> So the LORD scattered them from there over all the earth, and they stopped building the city. That is why it was called Babel—because there the LORD confused the language of the whole world. From there the LORD scattered them over the face of the whole earth.

• Why do you think the people built a tower? What was their goal?

- God could have stopped this tower in numerous ways. Why do you think he chose to confuse the language of these people?

- Do you see the confusing of the people's language as positive or negative? Why?

MY THOUGHTS

One language, one speech, one tower: to our ears, this sounds like a utopia where immigration debates and racism could become distant flickers of the past. United by one purpose and ambition, all become capable of whatever they set out to do. The possibilities are endless. When all people unite together in one nation, there's nowhere to go but up.

But before we buy into a utopian scenario for the people of Babel, we need to remind ourselves that within most empires a social hierarchy exists that creates the haves and have-nots. The dreams of the first Babylonians most likely came from certain leaders possessing a higher concentration of power. They wanted to advance their own names rather than glorify God. We can only guess where the commoners would have ended up if this movement had continued unchecked.

From our perspective in the United States, we might assume that this united group had a good thing going. If only they hadn't tried to challenge God by making a name for themselves. We might even see this as a tragic story of opportunity lost, a potential golden age squandered on a lousy building project.

However, second and third world theologians see this story differently. To the people who feel oppressed by wealthier nations, the unity of one language and one speech can be seen as creating the potential to squash diversity under the grand plans of the few in power. By scattering this unified group of Babylonians, God ensured a certain degree of diversity by spreading the fish of the large pond into a series of smaller ponds. Oppression is still possible within smaller groups but not to the same degree.

I was suspicious of this interpretation when I first ran into it. After all, isn't the account of the Tower of Babel just a story about challenging the authority and power of God? In fact, I hardly even sniffed the scent of racism, class struggle, or oppression. Are third world theologians reading in their own context? Or am I inserting my own context into this story? It's easy to accuse others of tinkering with the text when my own interpretations aren't challenged by an outside perspective. The truth is that everyone colors the biblical text to one degree or another.

Still, the interpretation of the Tower of Babel as God pitted against the pride of humanity and the backstory of oppression can coexist. Social overtones are present in Scripture that we can miss if we're not observant. While we can't speak conclusively about what exactly happened in Babel, human history and our own observations about human nature should tell us that we at least need to listen to the way second and third world theologians see and interpret these events.

INSIGHTS FROM THE HISTORIC/GLOBAL CHURCH

Jose Miguez-Bonino, Emeritus Professor of Systematic Theology and Ethics at Instituto Superior Evangélico de Estudios Teológicos, wrote the short study of Genesis 11:1-9 that first opened my eyes to the wonderful benefit of including global theologians with reflection on Scripture. After briefly describing the cultural atmosphere of Ecuador in the wake of the conquistadors, he moves on to present an analysis of Genesis 11 from his particular place in the world. Miguez-Bonino says:

> The purpose of this passage, therefore, is *not* primarily the expla-
> nation of the origin of diverse languages, *but* the condemnation
> and defeat of the imperial arrogance and universal domination

represented by the symbol of Babylon. God's action, then, is two-fold: the thwarting of the project of the false unity of domination *and* the liberation of the nations that possess their own places, languages, and families. The punishment of imperial Babylon is simultaneously the liberation of diverse nations.[2]

APPLYING TO MISSION

- Have you ever overlooked the needs of another social group or person different from yourself? How does the story of the Tower of Babel apply to these kinds of situations?

- Look up a mission organization such as Wycliffe or World Team and examine the way they handle the complexities of Christianity as they work in other cultures of the world.

- Propose three ways you can form theology with other Christians around you. How could you even include the voices of Christians from other cultures? Apply one of these over the next week.

LIVING OUT YOUR THEOLOGY

- Are there any dangers associated with including global theologians in our local theologies? Explain.

- In what ways does your culture help or hinder your theology?

Session 10

THE JOINING OF SPIRIT AND TRUTH

To get the most out of this session,
I suggest reading chapter 11 in Coffeehouse Theology.

Theology is practical. There's no such thing as theology without a practical element. Even if we don't want theology to affect how we live, it will. Some of the world's worst atrocities have been committed by people who believed that God was on their side, while other ghastly acts have been perpetrated by countries who believe that no God exists to stop them. Whether we rope God in or lock him out of our schemes, we'll always find that our theologies are significant.

The most important decision we face is whether we will worship God and if we will do so within the bounds of Christian orthodoxy—the accepted and essential beliefs of the Christian church. Our beliefs shape our lives, especially our beliefs that influence who and how we worship. Theology isn't an end in and of itself. Rather it's the servant of Christians who use it as a tool for knowing and worshipping God.

CONTEXT: THEOLOGY IN THE LIFE OF THE CHURCH

American theologians David Wells and Mark Noll lamented the state of evangelical theology in the 1990s, claiming that an anti-intellectual culture had crept into their corner of the church. Whether or not we agree with Wells and Noll, it's pretty safe to say that while theology influences how we live, Christians certainly need to pay more attention to the formation of these beliefs. Sermons, small groups, and Bible studies have done well to some degree, but discussion groups can't replace critical theological discussion that takes into account our context, historical traditions, and global Christians.

In fact, in the wake of a report[1] on the state of his church and several others, Bill Hybels, pastor of Willow Creek Community Church, shared, "We should have started telling people and teaching people that they have to take responsibility to become 'self feeders.' We should have gotten people, taught people, how to read their Bible between services."[2] In other words, one of the most connected pastors in America openly acknowledges that Christians are acutely aware of their own need to become better students of the Bible. What's more, Hybels is now working on ways to help Christians become not only fully devoted followers of Christ, but also fully committed theologians. Of course, we all face the challenge of keeping in mind the complexities of our context and the perspectives of Christians from history and around the world.

With this context in mind, ponder and discuss the following questions:

- How can understanding theology as an ongoing conversation change the way we form theology?

- Discuss ways that Christians can balance a pursuit of theological truth with Christ's command to love one another.

- Has theology ever been destructive to Christian unity for you? How could you have prevented it?

MEDITATION

Take some time to meditate on John 4:23-24 and then discuss the questions that follow:

> Yet a time is coming and has now come when the true worshippers will worship the Father in spirit and truth, for they are the kind of worshipers the Father seeks. God is spirit, and his worshipers must worship in spirit and in truth.

- What does it mean to worship God in spirit and in truth?

- What do you think happens when we lose balance and emphasize one over the other?

MY THOUGHTS

While struggling to sing hymns at the wedding of my wife's college room-mate, I had a profound revelation about worshipping God. Due to my inability to sight-read the notes dotted across the hymnal, I felt completely lost.

Meanwhile, the wedding party—most of whom sang professionally or at least in serious choirs on the side—belted out their assigned parts with broad smiles. After spending so much of my time arguing that hymns are dated and need to be shelved, I realized that most of my dislike for hymns is rooted in my own musical deficiencies. I regularly led worship with contemporary worship songs that relied on repetition and simple chord patterns, and I'm sure the traditionalists in my church winced every time I botched a hymn on Sunday morning (and that happened a lot . . . more times than I care to mention).

I finally realized that my preoccupation with the particulars of the music and lyrics took the place of the actual spiritual practice of worshipping God. And I left that wedding ceremony with a newfound appreciation for hymns, realizing that different forms of worship can exist when the object of the worship is correct and the content is grounded in truth.

How easily we can be sidetracked by fruitless arguments: hymns vs. contemporary songs, Gerazim vs. Jersusalem. Like the woman Jesus spoke the words of John 4 to, we often cloud the larger issues about our sins and the business of truly worshipping God. Instead of digging into the pressing matters of her own heart, this woman tried to distract Jesus with a question as useless as asking where to put the altar or pulpit for a church service.

Jesus began to speak the hard truth into her life while accepting her where she was: an outcast from society, living with a man outside of marriage. Since the Jews of Jesus' day sometimes stoned women for such offenses against God's law, she was getting off comparatively easy with her lonely trek to the well in the heat of the day. Jesus cut through taboos and gave her a chance to know and worship God, but she countered with a well-worn argument about the particulars of worship: which mountain is approved by God? This was a smart move for a woman who wanted to cover her tracks.

But Jesus cut right to the chase and proclaimed what God really wants. It turns out that God cares a lot about two things we often sacrifice on the altars of our debates. He's most interested in people committed to spirit and truth. The spirit part refers to the otherworldly nature of God and the level he desires to meet his people on. God reaches out, making it possible for people to receive his spirit and worship in this way. But we have to leave our own agendas and preferences behind, whether they include a mountain, hymnal, or acoustic guitar.

When Jesus talks to this Samaritan woman about the truth, he's likely taking a dig at the theological errors of the Samaritan people that limited the accepted Scriptures to only the first five books of the Torah. In addition, Jesus might also be hinting at the woman's attempt to hide her tattered past earlier in their conversation. From either angle, Jesus makes it abundantly clear that truth is another key in worshipping a spiritual God. In this brief moment, Jesus bumps up worship to a higher level, essentially rendering the traditional system of temple worship and worship tied directly to a geographical location null and void.

So what does this passage imply as we form and practice theology today? First, we can't forget the simple truth that God is spirit, and so the Holy Spirit must be included when we deal with him. God desires us to meet him on the spiritual level. Theology that builds an idle arsenal of knowledge is a poor excuse for Christian theology.

Second, theology that is honest, personal, and informed must be tied deeply to the truth of God. Just as the Samaritans didn't quite know who they were worshipping, even the most spiritual among us can fall off track and miss out on the truth of God. This is where theology can truly serve the church, grounding spiritual worship with the truth of God.

INSIGHTS FROM THE HISTORIC/GLOBAL CHURCH

In addition to contributing the commentary on the gospel of John to *The IVP Women's Bible Commentary*, Kamila A. Blessing is the vice president for congregational ministries and director of the incubation center for congregational resources, Christian Board of Publications, St. Louis, Missouri. In her approach to John 4, she deftly draws attention to the previous chapter, with Nicodemus and his stealthy questions for Jesus. Blessing compares the effect Jesus had on Nicodemus with his effect on this woman, whom he confronts with a message about true worship. In her final analysis, Blessing states:

> The only pronouncement of Jesus' messiahship and an implicit
> identification of the Messiah with God is made to a woman, a

non-Jew and a person of earthly disrepute, rather than to one of his own — because she is thirsty for that knowledge.

In contrast to Nicodemus, the Samaritan woman goes into the city and brings her fellow Samaritans to faith in Jesus. The story closes with the Samaritans' declaration that they now believe because of Jesus rather than the woman's testimony alone. They alone in the Gospel call him "the Savior of the world . . ."

Thus this woman is fruitful for Christ, whereas Nicodemus is not. She contrasts with other disciples also because she enters into a theological discussion with Jesus. Characteristically in John, the male disciples are passively present; they fail in persistence; they leave the tomb upon finding it empty; and they fail to speak their mind to Jesus. This woman may be regarded as one of the sowers whose planting the other disciples are to reap. In a powerful way, one that defies social convention, she carries out the functions of a true disciple.[3]

APPLYING TO MISSION

• What two ideas in this study guide or in *Coffeehouse Theology* have you found most helpful?

• How can you put these ideas into practice on a regular basis?

• List at least three ways you can increase your theological discussions with other Christians.

LIVING OUT YOUR THEOLOGY

- Read a popular magazine or newspaper related to your town or nation and write down five observations about your context that it reveals.

- Communications theorist Marshall McLuhan said, "The medium is the message." What are the media used in your culture and what do they teach you about it? What are the ramifications for theology?

- Read John 3–4 and compare Nicodemus to the woman at the well. How do their scenarios and responses relate to the imagery and symbols of John's gospel of light and dark?

NOTES

GETTING STARTED

1. *Wikipedia* contributors, "Culture," *Wikipedia: The Free Encyclopedia*, http://en.wikipedia.org/wiki/Culture. *Wikipedia* is an online encyclopedia written collaboratively by volunteers from around the world. While people in the academic world might question *Wikipedia* as a source, I've used this definition here because it provides an excellent snapshot of both traditional and current thought regarding what defines culture.

2. Augustine, quoted in L. Gregory Jones, *The Art of Reading Scripture*, eds. Ellen F. Davis and Richard B. Hays (Grand Rapids, MI: Eerdmans, 2003), 154.

SESSION 1

1. N. T. Wright, *What Saint Paul Really Said: Was Paul of Tarsus the Real Founder of Christianity?* (Grand Rapids, MI: Eerdmans, 1997), 153–157.

2. Helen R. Graham, "Acts 2:1-42. An Asian Perspective," *Return to Babel: Global Perspectives on the Bible*, eds. John R. Levinson and Priscilla Pope-Levinson (Louisville, KY: Westminster John Knox, 1999), 173–179.

SESSION 2

1. Irenaeus, "Irenaeus on the Role of Tradition," *The Christian Theology Reader*, ed. Alister E. McGrath (Oxford: Blackwell, 1998), 44.

SESSION 3

1. George R. Hunsberger, "Missional Vocation: Called and Sent to Represent the Reign of God," *Missional Church: A Vision for the Sending of the Church in North America,* Darrell L. Guder, ed. (Grand Rapids, MI: Eerdmans, 1998), 87.
2. My thanks to Brian McLaren for introducing me to this particular phrase.
3. The deuterocanonical books of 1 and 2 Maccabees can be found in the Catholic and Orthodox Bibles.
4. N. T. Wright, *Jesus and the Victory of God* (Minneapolis, MN: Augsburg Fortress, 1997), 505.
5. Wright, 506.
6. Wright, 507.

SESSION 4

1. Since everything in chapters 4 and 5 is devoted to explaining our context, it is superfluous to frame the context chapter within another discussion about context.
2. Christians rarely consider the ramifications of God's overlooking the ignorance of the Gentiles before the arrival of the gospel. This hints that grace does exist outside of the gospel, but this is not the place to jump into an issue requiring a whole book in and of itself.
3. N. T. Wright, *The Resurrection of the Son of God* (Minneapolis, MN: Augsburg Fortress, 2003), 32-38.
4. William A. Dyrness, *Learning About Theology from the Third World* (Grand Rapids, MI: Zondervan, 1990), 57.

SESSION 5

1. Brian McLaren, *More Ready Than You Realize: The Power of Everyday Conversation* (Grand Rapids, MI: Zondervan, 2000), 14.
2. Craig Van Gelder, "Missional Context: Understanding North American Culture," *Missional Church: A Vision for the Sending of the Church in North America*, ed. Darrell L. Guder (Grand Rapids, MI: Eerdmans, 1998), 8.

3. For additional study, see also Hosea 13:14; Luke13:11-16; Colossians 2:14-15; Ephesians 6:12; Hebrews 2:14-18; 1 John 3:7-10.

4. In his book *Ancient-Future Faith: Rethinking Evangelicalism for a Postmodern World* (Grand Rapids, MI: Baker, 1999), Robert Webber, a central theologian in the emerging church, spends a great deal of time relating Christus Victor to the needs of our society today.

5. Irenaeus, "Irenaeus on the 'Ransom' Theory of Atonement," *The Christian Theology Reader*, ed. Alister E. McGrath (Oxford: Blackwell, 1998), 176.

SESSION 6

1. As the secular governments of Western nations interact with nations in the Middle East, where religion is closely linked to politics, some diplomats are finding that we simply cannot ignore religion when trying to solve global problems. See the story of Douglas Johnston: "Diplomacy and Religion in the Twenty-First Century," *Speaking of Faith*, January 3, 2008, http://speakingoffaith.publicradio.org/programs/diplomacyandreligion/index.shtml.

2. Former Arkansas governor Mike Huckabee repeatedly referred to the Bible during his campaign for the Republican presidential nomination in 2008, but some wondered if people really knew what he was talking about. A report on NPR revealed that many people didn't. See Barbara Bradley Hagerty, "The Gospel According to Mike Huckabee," *All Things Considered*, February 8, 2008, http://www.npr.org/templates/story/story.php?storyId=18821021.

3. See Dan Kimball's book *They Like Jesus but Not the Church: Insights from Emerging Generations* (Grand Rapids, MI: Zondervan, 2007).

4. Of course I'm proving my own point here by using Paul as an example of relying on God's power.

5. N. T. Wright, *The Resurrection of the Son of God* (Minneapolis, MN: Augsburg Fortress, 2003), 285.

SESSION 7

1. Roger Olson, *The Story of Christian Theology: Twenty Centuries of Tradition and Reform* (Downers Grove, IL: InterVarsity, 1999), 538–589.

2. I admit that this requires a little bit of fancy theological footwork. In one sense, the Jewish Messiah didn't necessarily have to be God. But when this passage is reinterpreted by Peter, it would seem that we need to read back a Trinitarian understanding, Jesus the Lord is speaking with God the Father, YHWH.

3. Lesslie Newbigin, *The Gospel in a Pluralist Society* (Grand Rapids, MI: Eerdmans, 1989), 117.

SESSION 8

1. Richard B. Hayes, *The Moral Vision of the New Testament: Community, Cross, New Creation, a Contemporary Introduction to New Testament Ethics* (San Francisco: HarperSanFrancisco, 1996), 100.

SESSION 9

1. See *Christianity Today's* Christian Vision Project: www.christianvisionproject .com.

2. Jose Miguez-Bonino, "Genesis 11:1-9, A Latin American Perspective," *Return to Babel*, eds. John R. Levinson and Priscilla Pope-Levinson (Louisville, KY: Westminster John Knox, 1999), 15.

SESSION 10

1. See Greg Hawkins and Cally Parkinson, *Reveal: Where Are You?* (Willow Creek Association, 2007). Greg Hawkins is the executive pastor of Willow Creek Community Church.

2. Mike Rucker, "Willow Creek Repents?" Out of Ur, October 18, 2007, http://blog.christianitytoday.com/outofur/archives/2007/10/willow_creek_re.html.com/outofur/archives/2007/10/willow_creek_re.html.

3. Kamilla A. Blessing, "John," *The IVP Women's Bible Commentary* (Downers Grove, IL: InterVarsity, 2002), 598–599.

ABOUT THE AUTHOR

ED CYZEWSKI (MDiv, Biblical Theological Seminary) works in the nonprofit sector of southwest Vermont and as a freelance writer. He has served as the chair and communications chair of the Northshire Nonprofit Network, a group of nonprofits committed to nonprofit collaboration, education, and advocacy. He serves with several ministries and nonprofit organizations in Vermont, and volunteers with Shevet Achim, a Christian organization dedicated to bringing Arab children to Israeli hospitals for life-saving surgery. He blogs regularly on theology at http://inamirrordimly.com and on writing at www.edcyz.com.

Don't forget to check out the Coffeehouse Theology book and discussion guide!

Coffeehouse Theology

Ed Cyzewski

978-1-60006-277-3

1-60006-277-6

A relationship with God is central to life-breathing theology, but today's culture experiences a barrier of ignorance and misunderstanding of the church's mission. Through stories and illustrations, Ed Cyzewski builds a method for theology that is rooted in a relationship with God and his mission.

Coffeehouse Theology Contemporary Issues Discussion Guide

Ed Cyzewski

978-1-60006-299-5

1-60006-299-7

This conversational guide to theology in the postmodernism context and in the emerging church helps you understand, shape, and live out practical Christian theology.

The Message//Remix: Solo

978-1-60006-105-9

1-60006-105-2

In *Coffeehouse Theology*, Ed references *The Message//Remix: SOLO*, an innovative devotional designed to change how you interact with God's Word. *The Message Remix: Solo* revolves around lectio divina, or "divine reading," an ancient approach to exploring Scripture.

To order copies, visit your local Christian bookstore, call NavPress at 1-800-366-7788, or log on to www.navpress.com.
To locate a Christian bookstore near you, call 1-800-991-7747.

WWW.NOTFORSALECAMPAIGN.ORG

Not for Sale is a campaign of students, entrepreneurs, artists, people of faith, athletes, law enforcement officers, politicians, social workers, skilled professionals, and all justice seekers, united to fight the global slave trade.

Not for Sale aims to educate and mobilize an international abolitionist movement through the innovation and implementation of open-source activism. Inside the United States, the campaign identifies trafficking rings and collaborates with local law enforcement and community groups to shut them down and provide support for the victims. Internationally, the campaign partners with poorly resourced abolitionist groups to enhance their capacity.

Every single person has a skill that they can give to free an individual living in bondage.

Here's a resource
to help you pray
with more

Power,
Passion,
& Purpose

Every issue of *Pray!* brings you:

- **Special Themes** that deal with specific, often groundbreaking topics of interest that will help you grow in your passion and effectiveness in prayer
- **Features** on important and intriguing aspects of prayer, both personal and corporate
- **Ideas** to stimulate creativity in your prayer life and in the prayer life of your church
- **Empowered**: a special section written by church prayer leaders, for church prayer leaders
- **Prayer News** from around the world, to get you up-to-date with what God is doing through prayer all over the globe

- **Prayer Journeys**: a guest-authored column sharing how God moved him or her closer to Jesus through prayer
- **Intercession Ignited**: providing encouragement, inspiration, and insight for people called to the ministry of intercession
- **Classics**: featuring time-tested writings about prayer from men and women of God through the centuries
- **Inspiring Art** from a publication that has been recognized nationally for its innovative approach to design
- **And much, much more!**

No Christian who wants to connect more deeply with God
should be without *Pray!*

Six issues of *Pray!* are only $21.97*

Canadian and international subscriptions are only $29.97 (Includes Canadian GST).

*plus sales tax where applicable